Deception and Financial Mayhem

T0413239

Deception and Financial Mayhem

The Promise of Blockchain Technology

Faisal Sheikh and Saad Maniar

BUSINESS EXPERT PRESS

Leader in applied, concise business books

Deception and Financial Mayhem: The Promise of Blockchain Technology

Copyright © Business Expert Press, LLC, 2025

Cover design by Karl Moeller

Interior design by Exeter Premedia Services Private Ltd., Chennai, India

All rights reserved. No part of this publication may be reproduced, stored in a retrieval system, or transmitted in any form or by any means—electronic, mechanical, photocopy, recording, or any other except for brief quotations, not to exceed 400 words, without the prior permission of the publisher.

First published in 2025 by
Business Expert Press, LLC
222 East 46th Street, New York, NY 10017
www.businessexpertpress.com

ISBN-13: 978-1-63742-760-6 (paperback)
ISBN-13: 978-1-63742-761-3 (e-book)

Business Expert Press Financial Accounting, Auditing, and Taxation Collection

First edition: 2025

10 9 8 7 6 5 4 3 2 1

EU SAFETY REPRESENTATIVE
Mare Nostrum Group B.V.
Mauritskade 21D
1091 GC Amsterdam
The Netherlands
gpsr@mare-nostrum.co.uk

We dedicate this book to the future of the audit profession, to the unsung auditors who safeguard the integrity of financial statements and ensure the smooth functioning of global markets.

Description

Deception and Financial Mayhem **explores whether the corporate psychopath accountant can be identified, modeled, and ultimately constrained.**

This book extensively discusses accounting fraud, including recent accounting scandals, and its relationship with corporate governance. Major accounting fraud models, including the fraud triangle, are examined, and the lens of *the dark triad (Machiavellianism, narcissism, and psychopathy)* is also presented to better understand the perpetrators of accounting fraud.

Utilizing the Levenson's self-report psychopathy scale, a multiple regression model known as the "**corporate psychopath equation**" is proposed to potentially identify psychopathic tendencies in accountants and auditors. The foundational aspects of blockchain technology are covered along with its potential to prevent accounting fraud.

The authors outline automation technologies and "people-centric approaches," including the **Sheikh Maniar Anti-Fraud Culture Builder**—which can potentially foster an ethical culture and deter accounting fraud until blockchain technology becomes ubiquitous. Finally, perpetual vigilance is advised, even as the specter of the corporate psychopath accountant may diminish.

Contents

Foreword 1

The opening sentence in Faisal and Saad's book sends a shiver down my spine.

"The authors argue that Accounting Fraud continues and has become an almost accepted feature of the business environment." I feel I must make the point that it is not the role of the external auditors to detect fraud. It will always be the case though that when financial scandals occur, as they will, questions are asked of everyone, and that will include the auditors. And such questions are never good for our profession.

I was flattered to be asked by Faisal to write a forward for his new book "Deception and Financial Mayhem."

I am an Executive Partner at Beever and Struthers, a UK-based firm of chartered accountants and business advisors. My day-job is an audit partner, having been in the profession now for over 30 years.

As a firm we first met Faisal several years ago, as we introduced placement year students into our audit teams. Faisal's care and attention, helping his students take those first steps into practice, were invaluable in making this program a success (that continues to this day).

We realized as a firm that working closely with academics with their focus on the audit profession and change management would help us think differently, and question what has always been done. It is comforting to read the conclusions Faisal and Saad have reached in this book. That automation and "people-centric" approaches are the keystones to a fit-for-purpose audit in today's environment. But I have sped to the end of the book, I should really start at the beginning.

Anyone who has spent any time with me knows that *curiosity* is my favorite word. It is the characteristic I value over any other. With curiosity comes professional skepticism, and with that comes the best audits.

Before reading this book, I took some time out to revisit Faisal Sheikh's previous book "When Numbers Don't Add Up." In this book Faisal lifted the veil covering the murky world of accounting fraud, and introduced the world of blockchain, Big Data and the use of data-analytic tools within audit as means to introduce a new age of financial control.

My colleague, Richard Williams, penned a forward to this earlier book, and ended with the statement that as "a profession we stand on the threshold of a new age of financial control, replacing sample-base substantive and even controls-based audit techniques with computer-assisted audit tools. It feels that as a profession we are still balanced, a little precariously, at the top of that transformation curve." Faisal and Saad's new book concludes with the assertion that introducing automation to the audit and focusing on people-centric approaches are the way to minimize accounting fraud. This is music to my ears. It rings true with all we as an audit firm, and indeed the wider profession, are looking to achieve, and must surely be the nudge required to encourage our colleagues to make those changes.

Auditors around the world are comfortable with the concept of the Fraud Triangle. This features, in some way or other, in our working papers where, as required by the auditing standards, we identify and address the potential risks of material misstatement in financial statements due fraud and misrepresentation, and design audit procedures to respond to such risks.

In this book Faisal and Saad raise the bar and introduces the concept of the *corporate psychopath* or *corporate psychopath accountant.* When Faisal first introduced his idea to me, I must admit I was taken apart. More so when I read the statistics Faisal and Saad have included in their explanation of the concept. Have I really come across so many psychopaths through my 30+ years in the auditing profession? It would seem inevitable that I have. And that brings us to the crux of the problem for the auditor. Faisal and Saad neatly sum this up; "management override is viewed as the "Achilles's heel" of fraud prevention…."

As companies produce more and more data, auditors, particularly tech-savvy ones, have the ability to consider multiple financial and non-financial factors, to form fuller, more rounded, insights into the operations of the operations, and so better challenge assertions put forward by finance teams. This represents a huge change in our audit process, as Faisal and Saad mention, moving to "correlation rather than causation."

Faisal and Saad drill into the solutions blockchain technology can bring to the audit profession in more detail in this book, inevitable as our knowledge deepens. But this still feels a step too far for the general profession today.

Much more achievable are the alternative options Faisal and Saad presents at the end of his book, with a focus on automation and a "people-centric" approach. This will require a change in mindset for the audit profession, as we head into an environment for which we are generally ill-equipped now.

We will need to reconsider the skillset we require within an audit team. Our audit teams must now include data analysts, supported by data engineers to structure the plethora of data we have available to us. This will only grow in importance. And who knows, perhaps as I reluctantly accept I am becoming one of the grey-haired people in the room I will still be able to experience an environment where we can audit in real-time, a concept I was first introduced to some ten years before talking to a Scandinavian team of auditors already working in such a way!

For now, I will simply ask all our auditors to read Faisal and Saad's book, with two objectives in mind; remember the possibility we are dealing with a corporate psychopath or corporate psychopath accountant and keep curious! Exciting times indeed!

—Caroline Monk, Executive partner
Beever and Struthers, United Kingdom (beeverstruthers.co.uk)

Foreword 2

In the intricate world of financial reporting, where transparency and trust are paramount, "Deception and Financial Mayhem: The Promise of Blockchain Technology" emerges as a beacon of innovation and hope. The authors, Dr. Faisal Sheikh and Saad Maniar, have crafted a masterpiece that not only dissects the pernicious issues of accounting fraud but also offers groundbreaking solutions through the application of innovative tech including big data and Blockchain Technology (BCT).

I was struck by authors' profound understanding of the multifaceted nature of financial fraud. Their ability to illuminate the dark corners of corporate malfeasance and propose tangible solutions is nothing short of remarkable. This research-backed book is a testament to their expertise and vision, and it is a privilege to introduce this essential read to you.

The book begins by meticulously examining the persistent problem of accounting fraud, a scourge that has long plagued the financial industry. By exploring the psychological underpinnings of corporate fraudsters, specifically the "Dark Triad" of Machiavellianism, Narcissism, and Psychopathy, the authors provide invaluable insights into the minds of those who perpetrate these crimes. Their development of the "Corporate Psychopath Equation" is a pioneering tool that offers a predictive framework for identifying high-risk individuals in corporate environments. As noted by the authors it is the first time in the literature that accounting/audit practitioners were tested for psychopathy, and I am sure the model will be refined over time with better explanatory variables that will enhance the variability of the model.

However, it is the authors' exploration of Blockchain Technology (BCT) that truly sets this book apart. Blockchain (BC), often heralded as the next technological revolution, is presented here not just as a buzzword but as a practical and transformative tool for the auditing profession. The authors' thorough analysis of BC's capabilities—its immutability, transparency, and decentralized nature—illustrates how it can fundamentally alter the landscape of financial reporting.

In a world where traditional auditing methods are increasingly challenged by sophisticated fraud schemes, BC offers a robust alternative. The immutable ledger created by BCT ensures that once a transaction is recorded, it cannot be altered or deleted. This feature alone provides an unprecedented level of security and trust. By leveraging BC, auditors can ensure that financial records are accurate and tamper-proof, significantly reducing the risk of fraud.

Moreover, the concept of continuous auditing enabled by BC is a game-changer. Traditional audits, which are often periodic and retrospective, can miss ongoing fraudulent activities. BC's real-time data recording allows for continuous monitoring, enabling auditors to detect and address irregularities as they occur. This shift from periodic audits to continuous assurance could drastically enhance the integrity of financial reporting.

The authors also delve into the practical challenges and opportunities of implementing BC in auditing. They discuss the need for collaboration between technologists and auditors, the importance of regulatory support, and the necessity for training and education to equip auditors with the skills needed to navigate this new landscape. Their vision of a future where BCT is seamlessly integrated into the auditing process is both compelling and achievable.

Beyond the technical aspects, the book emphasizes the broader implications of BC for corporate governance and ethical behavior. By promoting transparency and accountability, BC can help foster a corporate culture where ethical behavior is the norm, not the exception. The authors argue convincingly that the adoption of BCT could lead to a significant reduction in financial fraud, benefiting not just individual companies but the economy. On the other hand, as acknowledged by the authors the merits and advantages would only be fruitful if the tech becomes adopted at large, which is not the case right now. However, they correctly point out that until BCT becomes ubiquitous automation is the preparation or forerunner for this nascent tech.

The modern world is already taking a leap of faith towards intangible assets and a substantial share of economy is now based on these intellectual property rights. Engine of our economic growth has begun shifting from goods and services to intangible assets. Complexity is growing around recognition, measurement and reporting of these assets. Borders are becoming irrelevant with freedom to operate in several jurisdictions through patents and intellectual property. Digitization is transforming the fundamental makeup of global economy. During these times, the authors are advocating about what role the profession is meant to play in this exciting—and controversial—space.

"Deception and Financial Mayhem" is more than a scholarly text; it is a clarion call for the auditing profession to embrace innovation. The authors' meticulous research and forward-thinking solutions make this book an indispensable resource for auditors, accountants, regulators, and anyone committed to enhancing the integrity of financial reporting.

As you embark on this enlightening journey, I encourage you to reflect on the profound implications of the insights presented. The future of accounting and auditing hinges on our ability to adapt and innovate. This book provides a roadmap to a future where financial integrity is upheld by the transformative power of BCT.

—M. Jameel Hussain Khan BCom, MEcon, FCA (ICAP),
CPA (Cañada) CFO Marina Homes Inc. (Cañada)

Acknowledgments

Saad and I are deeply grateful for the collaborative efforts that made this book possible to our families and colleagues for their unwavering support and constant good humor. We extend special thanks to Caroline and Jameel for graciously taking the time from their busy schedules to craft such insightful and thought-provoking forewords. Their unique perspectives—as an audit partner and CFO—bring valuable insights from distinct yet equally important vantage points.

We remain ever appreciative of Business Expert Press for embracing this project and supporting us in pushing the boundaries of accounting and audit knowledge. This work is grounded in fintech solutions such as Blockchain Technology and Automation, with a "people-centric" approach to tackling issues like accounting fraud and the corporate psychopath phenomenon, including the corporate psychopath accountant.

We leave you with the often-quoted saying, *"Accounting is the language of business,"* by Warren Buffett. Saad and I believe this statement underscores the foundational role of accounting. Mastering and evolving this "language" is essential for understanding and advancing the business world. It implies that by pushing the boundaries of accounting knowledge, we can unlock deeper insights and drive innovation across various industries.

We remain students....

January 2025
Faisal and Saad

CHAPTER 1

What Is Accounting Fraud and Why It Persists

> *If you see fraud and do not say fraud, you are a fraud.*
> —Nassim Nicolas Taleb, Author of the acclaimed Black
> Swan and other important books

The authors argue that accounting fraud continues and has become an almost accepted feature of the business environment. Consequently, this study aims to explore whether there is a relationship between personality types as per the dark triad (psychopathy, narcissism, Machiavelli) focusing specifically on psychopathy and the rationalization of accounting fraud. Also, whether the nascent blockchain technology, automation, and people-centric' approaches can dampen if not eradicate accounting fraud.

An individual who has a range of distinct personality traits and behavioral patterns is referred to as a psychopath. They are frequently distinguished by a lack of empathy, regret, and a diminished capacity to develop deep emotional connections with others. The *Diagnostic and Statistical Manual of Mental Disorders (DSM-5)*—the standard reference used by mental health practitioners to diagnose mental disorders—does not explicitly recognize psychopathy as a clinical diagnosis. However, it is frequently used in everyday speech and is connected to the *DSM-5* diagnosis known as antisocial personality disorder (ASPD).

Common traits linked to psychopaths or people with ASPD include the following:

1. **Lack of empathy:** Psychopaths frequently find it difficult to relate to or comprehend the feelings and experiences of others.

They might struggle to understand other people's emotions and behave appropriately, which could cause them to be disrespectful of other people's rights and well-being.

2. **Superficial charm and manipulation:** Psychopaths frequently have the capacity to charm and influence others to further their own objectives. They could be good at donning a charming or likable persona but lack true empathy or care.

3. **Impulsivity and irresponsible behavior:** Psychopaths frequently act impulsively and irresponsibly without considering the potential repercussions for themselves or others.

4. **Lack of remorse:** Even when they cause injury or suffering to others, they frequently lack true regret or shame for their acts. They could blame others or lessen the effects of their acts by rationalizing or justifying their behavior.

5. **Deficient emotional intelligence:** Psychopaths frequently exhibit a limited emotional range or shallowness. They could find it challenging to maintain emotional bonds over time or even feel intense emotions such as love.

It is critical to remember that psychopathy is a complicated and divisive subject in psychology and psychiatry. Experts in the field continue to disagree about how it should be conceptualized, how to diagnose it, and whether it belongs on a spectrum or not. *It is also important to note that not everyone with psychopathic tendencies commits crimes or endangers other people.*

The phrase *corporate psychopath* describes a person who has psychopathic propensities in a professional or organizational environment. It defines people who have traits that are typical of psychopathy, like a lack of empathy, manipulativeness, and a disregard for moral and ethical considerations, but who largely display these traits in the context of their professional relationships and behavior.

Corporate psychopaths frequently succeed at traversing the corporate ladder and may be skilled at influencing people to further their own and their employers' interests. They are frequently motivated by self-interest, a desire for power, and the pursuit of achievement at the expense of others. Typical characteristics of corporate psychopaths include:

1. **Charm and charisma:** Corporate psychopaths frequently have a captivating personality that makes it easy for them to influence and control others. They might utilize their charm to build relationships, establish allies, and accomplish their goals.

2. **Absence of remorse and empathy:** Corporate psychopaths share the same low capacity for empathy as psychopaths in other circumstances. They might take advantage of and control subordinates and coworkers without feeling regretful about it.

3. **Manipulative behavior:** Corporate psychopaths are excellent manipulators who employ a range of techniques, including deceit, charm, and strategic networking, to further their own objectives. They frequently take advantage of others' flaws and shortcomings to seize dominance and control.

4. **Grandiose self-image:** Corporate psychopaths frequently exhibit narcissistic tendencies and an exaggerated feeling of self-importance. They may engage in self-promotion and self-aggrandizement to boost their reputation and influence inside the organization because they feel superior to others.

5. **Absence of accountability:** Corporate psychopaths frequently avoid taking credit for their deeds and may place the blame elsewhere when anything goes wrong. They could be adept at hiding their actions or evading punishment for their immoral or damaging actions.

It is important to remember that not everyone in powerful positions or with prosperous jobs is a corporate psychopath. The phrase refers to a particular subset of people who behave in a psychopathic manner while working in a business or organizational setting.

Before the authors attempt to model the corporate psychopath accountant, they will briefly explore why accounting fraud continues, explain how this phenomenon contrasts with fraud in general, outline some of the major accounting scandals of recent times, examine the interplay of accounting fraud with corporate governance and its socioeconomic fallout, and finally, discuss the motivations or drivers for this perverse behavior.

Why Accounting Fraud Endures?

To gain a deeper insight into why accounting fraud occurs, a thorough understanding of the concept is essential. Consequently, it is necessary to briefly explore the concept of white-collar crime, including corporate crime, which will give an overview of the phenomenon illustrated with important yet notorious accounting scandals such as Parmalat and the ensuing consequences. This will provide a basis for further exploration of the significance, nature, and cost of accounting fraud.

Thereafter, the authors will critically elaborate the important theoretical models of accounting fraud, beginning with the Donald Cressey's Fraud Triangle, including sociological and psychological approaches that attempt to explain why accounting fraud takes place.

Framework for Corporate Crime

As stated earlier, corporate crimes are white-collar crimes executed by corporations or an individual in a position of authority such as a CEO. This includes all corporate activities that are prohibited and punishable by law. It is argued that what is being sought are organizational benefits instead of individual gains. Many corporate crimes are highly complex, involving multiple actors, and it is difficult to establish who is responsible for the harm. It is likely that most ordinary people are unaware of the frequency and economic damage caused by corporate crimes. The socioeconomic fallout from criminal activities committed by companies can be devastating, resulting in tens of thousands of job losses, as in the case of WorldCom. It should not be a surprise when some commentators deem corporate crime to be one of the gravest crimes that occur in society.

It is argued that corporate crime wreaks more socioeconomic destruction than all street crime combined and is even claimed that corporate crime is a form of violent crime. Many social problems, such as tyranny of native and indigenous communities, food contamination, medical negligence, and unsafe working conditions, are a result of concerted corporate power. Furthermore, many of the penalties imposed on corporations have little or no impact on their finances and business practices; hence the requirement for alternative methods of restricting and effectively controlling corporate crime.

The authors will now focus on the understanding, modeling, and analysis of accounting fraud. Hence, there will also be an overview of the accounting fraud phenomenon, including a review of the most notorious accounting scandals of modern times as evidence of the socioeconomic impact of fraudulent financial reporting or accounting fraud.

What Is Fraud and How Accounting Fraud Is Unusual

Fraud has existed perhaps since the beginning of trade and commerce. According to Woodward et al. (2003), basic body measurements and calculations or biometrics were used thousands of years ago as a method of gauging the trustworthiness of traders, implying that dishonest businesspeople have always existed. In general, fraud includes the intent to deceive, breaking the rule of law or established norms or protocols such as accounting standards, resulting in negative, if not harmful, consequences to its victims. KPMG (2017a) noted that "[t]he total cost of fraudulent activity in the UK has surpassed a billion pounds (£1.1 billion) for the first time since 2011."

The *Oxford Dictionary* describes fraud in the following way:

Wrongful or criminal deception intended to result in financial or personal gain.

The above definition describes the fundamental nature of fraud but does not explain its nature and features. As already discussed, fraud is not a recent trend nor is it limited to humankind. Animals also engage in what could be argued, at minimum, as manipulative behavior, or fraudulent activities such as chameleons changing color. A more comprehensive definition of fraud is supplied by Van Vlasselaer et al. (2016):

Fraud is an uncommon, well-considered, imperceptibly concealed, time-evolving and often carefully organized crime which appears in many types of form.

We will now consider why we produce financial statements, and this will help to better explain why accounting fraud is different from fraud. Financial statements are prepared because they assist in decision making, planning, and controlling processes. In most of the world, it is also a statutory requirement to produce financial statements according to country-specific generally accepted accounting principles (GAAP) such as U.S. GAAP or International Financial Reporting Standards. Furthermore, the financial statements are vital tools for senior managers because they help to communicate past achievements and are a basis for future expectations or plans. The figures reported in the financial statements provide an important source of information regarding the evaluation of performance, going concern, and the story of the company's history. Thus, the accuracy of these documents is exceedingly important because they reflect the actual financial position of a company at any given time. External stakeholders such as analysts scrutinize the financial information supplied by financial statements to consider the financial performance of the company and make investments/recommendations accordingly. Specifically, equity investors and creditors will be concerned with the quality and sustainability of profitability and cash flow, these being the key sources of financing for the operation of the company. Financial statements for public listed companies are authenticated by both internal and external auditors to give more reliability to the reported financial position.

Jackson (2015) suggests that accounting fraud (also referred to as *corporate fraud* or *financial reporting fraud* or *financial statement fraud*) is a special kind of fraud that necessitates the manipulation of financial statements. It is argued that accounting fraud does not result in an explicit financial advantage to anyone. Instead, it supplies an implicit gain, in the shape of higher share prices, superior stock options for managers, and continued lines of credit.

The Association of Certified Fraud Examiners (ACFE) is a renowned American professional antifraud body that globally provides antifraud training and education. In the ACFEs 2018 *Fraud Examiners Manual*, accounting fraud is defined as "the deliberate misrepresentation of the financial condition of an enterprise accomplished through the intentional misstatement or omission of amounts or disclosures in the financial statements to deceive financial statement users." It is acknowledged that the first recorded example of accounting fraud was the one that occurred in the 1600s to the British East India Company.

Major corporate scandals have occurred that have shaken the confidence of all stakeholders, the public, and investors, and, worryingly in the financial system itself. The phenomenon of accounting fraud underpinned almost all cases of recent corporate scandals such as, the UK-based, Carillion in 2018. It is argued that when financial statements are not accurate because of accounting irregularities, they change from a highly useful tool into a way of deceiving the public.

Research suggests that unethical conduct and fraudulent activities such as manipulation of accounting information do not occur in a vacuum; rather, there must be specific factors that make it possible. It is maintained that most examples of corporate failure occur for various reasons, including fraudulent financial reporting, misuse of power, insider trading, corruption, bribery, unsuitable investment practices, pursuing short-term profits to the detriment of shareholders, poor internal control environment, and ineffective management.

Leading fraud examiners/analysts suggest that fraud is not merely an accounting problem but a social phenomenon and that there are three methods of unlawfully taking money from a victim, namely, by force, stealth, or trickery. Hence, a weak internal control environment in an organization is an opportunity for a fraudster. Where an accounting information system does not supply timely, accurate, sufficiently detailed, and relevant results, it is susceptible to theft and concealment from the company's bank account. A weak internal audit function, or lack of one, is also a sign of poor internal control. For example, a specific example of deficient accounting practice is failure to ensure monthly bank reconciliations.

The spectacular rise of corporate accounting scandals at the start of the 21st century has exacerbated the phenomenon of accounting fraud that causes corporate bankruptcy, unnecessary market corrections, and socioeconomic malaise. The following examples are the most notorious instances of accounting fraud scandals that highlight the unintended consequences of unethical behavior.

Enron, 2001

Enron Corporation, founded in 1985, was a large energy company that was engaged in an enormous fraudulent scheme that climaxed in 2001 when the company suffered the largest Chapter 11 bankruptcy in history (since exceeded by WorldCom during 2002 and Lehman Brothers during 2008).

Enron was a darling of the stock market and had been considered a blue-chip stock investment, so this was an unparalleled event in the financial world. Enron's passing occurred after the revelation that the bulk of its profits and revenue were the result of deals with special purpose entities. Thus, many of Enron's debts and the losses that it suffered were not reported in its financial statements, that is, accounting fraud. At the end of 2001, it was discovered that Enron's financial statements were underpinned by institutionalized, systematic, and creatively planned accounting fraud.

The main actors in the debacle were Chairman Jen Kay, CEO Jeffrey Skilling, and CFO Andrew Fastow, who engaged in highly aggressive off-balance sheet finance that resulted in billions of dollars in long-term debt being kept off the records. Ultimately, the figures did not correlate, and the inevitable decrease in net income led to an estimated billion-dollar reduction in the equity of shareholders. As expected, investors reacted negatively, and quickly Enron's stock price collapsed, from US$90.56 during the summer of 2000 to just pennies (January 11, 2002—$0.12), quickening the company's bankruptcy. It is estimated that Enron's shareholders lost nearly $74 billion, and 4,500 employees lost their jobs and pension funds without proper notice.

It is maintained that the fiasco could have been avoided if previous financial statements had been forensically examined. The remarkable revenue growth from $9.2 billion in 1995 to $100.8 billion in 2000 should have warned interested stakeholders that this was not underpinned by a similar increase in profitability.

The scandal highlighted aggressive accounting practices and activities of many corporations in the United States and was a major factor in the enactment of the Sarbanes–Oxley Act of 2002. The scandal also affected the wider business world by causing the closure of the renowned audit firm Arthur Andersen, which had been in business for nearly 100 years and was Enron's main auditor.

WorldCom, 2002

Less than a year after the financial earthquake caused by Enron, another scandal shook the markets in the telecommunication services supplier WorldCom, now known as MCI.

According to the U.S. Securities and Exchange Commission (SEC) (2003), the company's CEO Bernard Ebbers, CFO Scott Sullivan, Controller David Myers, and Director of General Accounting Buford Yates used duplicitous accounting techniques to conceal its decreasing earnings to maintain the price of WorldCom's share.

According to the literature, the fraud was executed by capitalizing rather than expensing approximately $3.8 billion of expenditure and inflating revenues with false accounting entries, creating an image of growth to exaggerate profits. The company filed for bankruptcy protection shortly after the revelation of the fraudulent scheme, causing 17,000 redundancies and losses of $180 billion.

Adelphia, 2002

Adelphia was a local cable franchise that was transformed by John Rigas into a giant of the telecommunications industry that included high-speed internet, cable, and long-distance telephone service. During May 2002, Adelphia declared earnings restatement for 2000 and 2001, which included billions of dollars in off-balance sheet liabilities linked with *co-borrowing agreements*. The financial statements of Adelphia highlighted a myriad of issues. According to the last 10 K filed by the company (for the year ended December 31, 2000), it showed a net loss of $548 million; of $21.5 billion in total assets, of which $14.1 billion were intangibles, liabilities totaled $16.3 billion, and equity was a modest $4.2 billion. Adelphia subsequently filed for bankruptcy in June 2002, after being investigated by the SEC, which resulted in company executives being charged with accounting fraud:

Adelphia, at the direction of the individual defendants: (1) fraudulently excluded billions of dollars of liabilities from its consolidated financial statements by hiding them in off-balance-sheet affiliates; (2) falsified operation statistics and inflated Adelphia's earnings to meet Wall Street expectations; and (3) concealed rampant self-dealing by the Rigas family (Gao 2002, 122).

At the heart of the accounting fraud were false transactions, with supporting documents suggesting that debts were repaid; instead, they were transferred to affiliates. In addition, the company was run as a personal fiefdom by the Rigas family, who, for example, used company funds to buy stock for the Rigas family and even built a golf club. It is important to note that five members of the nine-member board were John Rigas's immediate relatives, including his son, who was CFO, suggesting poor corporate governance and management override was potentially endemic in the company. Eventually, two former Adelphia executives were charged with criminal charges for conspiracy, bank fraud, and securities fraud. In 2004 John Rigas and his son were both convicted of conspiracy and fraud.

Global Crossing, 2002

Global Crossing was an integrated telecommunications solutions company that was founded in 1997 by an investment banker called Gary Winnick. Its headquarters were in Bermuda, but it operated primarily in the United States and 27 other countries and more than

200 cities across the globe. After a series of accounting indiscretions, the company announced Chapter 11 Bankruptcy Protection on January 28, 2002. Investors, analysts, and regulators were left stunned as Global Crossing was considered a darling of the market. The Chapter 11 statement also announced that two companies, namely, Hutchinson Whampoa and Singapore Technologies Telemedia, had signed a letter of intent that they would inject a $750 million cash investment in exchange for a combined majority share of 60 percent or more in the business.

A closer inspection of the financial statements revealed mounting debts of $12 billion coupled with unsecured creditors and affiliates numbering over one thousand. The latter covered a wide spectrum of lenders, equipment vendors, and other carriers. U.S. Trust Co., one of the secured creditors, was owed $3.6 billion, approximately 25 percent of Global Crossing's total debts. The company was highly valued on the market but had a poor cash flow and working capital position. The company had engaged in a dubious and complex earnings management technique, called "capacity swaps." Global Crossing would record traffic on other fiber-optic telecommunications systems such as QWEST and in return booked traffic on its own network. Thus, each counterparty in this complex accounting fraud reported an increase in recorded revenue, although there was no actual increase in economic activity. The swaps were also undertaken to conceal different costs and exceed market expectations. Global Crossing went on to lure more customers and investors by overstating the reach and attractiveness of its network. However, this was not underpinned by sound financials, including profitability and crucially cash flow, which is the lifeblood of any business. Consequently, Global Crossing became highly leveraged with unsustainable levels of liabilities coupled with questionable assets and became the largest telecom bankruptcy filing ever—the fourth largest of any kind in American corporate history. Unfortunately, the company was also plagued by poor governance, and even after its bankruptcy, it lent $15 million to John Legere, its then CEO, and, surprisingly, agreed to let him keep the money if he stayed on until February 2003.

Parmalat S.p.A, 2004

Parmalat S.p.A was an Italian multinational dairy and food company and at one time became the leading global producer of long-life milk, but the company folded in 2003 with a £13 billion hole in its financial statements in what remains Europe's biggest liquidation to date. The **SEC (2003)** described the European scandal as "one of the largest and most brazen corporate financial frauds in history." Parmalat was an example of accounting fraud that was achieved by several factors, including a weak corporate governance structure and lack of professional care by external auditors, and was exacerbated by the greed of senior management. Calisto Tanzi, founder, and CEO of Parmalat was prone to greed and unethical behavior, for example, redirecting Parmalat's monies to a company managed by his daughter, Francesca Tanzi (Ogutu 2016). An investigation reported that Tanzi diverted approximately €500 million to Permatour, a company that his daughter managed. Furthermore, it is suggested that what happened at Parmalat was premeditated and a flagrant misstatement of information with the intent to misinform.

It was reported that Parmalat defaulted on a $185 million bond payment in November 2002, causing its auditors and bankers to examine the company's consolidated accounts. This examination found that approximately 38 percent of company assets were allegedly held in a $4.9 billion Bank of America account of a company subsidiary in the Cayman Islands. However, in December 2002, the Bank of America reported that no account for this Parmalat subsidiary ever existed. Italian prosecutors stated that they had discovered that Parmalat management merely concocted assets to offset nearly $16.2 billion of liabilities and blatantly fabricated financial statements over a 15-year period, eventually driving Parmalat into insolvency.

Lehman Brothers, 2008

In 2008, Lehman Brothers filed for the largest Chapter 11 bankruptcy in history, with $639 billion in assets and $619 billion in debt. At the time, Lehman Brothers was the fourth-largest U.S. investment bank, and after its demise 25,000, employees globally lost their jobs.

It is suggested that legitimate accounting standards were misinterpreted coupled with accounting fraud to prepare and disclose financial statements according to the desire of Lehman Brother's senior management. Lehman Brothers did not show important transactions in the notes to the financial statements, causing some commentators to argue for the review of generally accepted accounting standards. At the crux of the accounting fraud was the aggressive employment of an accounting technique referred to as Repo 15 (Le Maux and Morin 2011, 42):

> On March 12, 2010, a 2,200-page enquiry report prepared by legal expert Anton R. Valukas revealed the extensive use of accounting manipulations that might have largely contributed to the collapse of Lehman Brothers, which went bankrupt on September 15, 2008. This report sheds light on the systematic use of a balance sheet window-dressing technique called Repo 105, which let Lehman remove approximately $50 billion in commitments from its balance sheet in June 2008, and artificially reduce its net debt level by wagering on the collateralized loan market.

It is claimed that Ernst & Young (EY) deliberately ignored balance sheet shenanigans as early as the early 2000s. If the cash flow statement had been analyzed, the accounting fraud could have been identified and potentially corrected.

Toshiba, 2015

In 2015, the CEO of Toshiba Corporation (Toshiba) resigned over the revelation of a JP¥151.8 billion Accounting Fraud (AF) that shocked the financial world. The accounting fraud was reported to be US$1.2 billion of earnings manipulation through window dressing; it later escalated to US$2 billion from 2008 to 2014.

Just like the Lehman 2008 scandal, legitimate accounting standards were abused to inflate revenue. Toshiba's operating profit was overstated by approximately US$4.1 billion from March 2012 to February 2015. This was due to the abuse of an accounting method called *percentage-of-completion*, which is routinely utilized in long-term projects. According to this method, sales and expenses are established in an accounting period completed to date. To deal with the intense media and public scrutiny, Toshiba set up a panel to investigate the extent of the accounting fraud. Toshiba asserted that the problem was caused by big civil engineering projects such as electricity generation and railways, where managers had decided on achieving profit targets by dishonestly reducing expenses. The managers' biased judgments, coupled with the knowledge of auditors, resulted in overstated sales and profits and corresponding understatements of expenses, including adjustments to goodwill. Toshiba continues to face class lawsuits from shareholders and the proud brand with a 140-year history lies in tatters.

Wirecard AG, 2020

Dubbed the *Enron of Germany*—Wirecard AG a Munich-based payments processor became insolvent in June 2020, at the height of the COVID-19 pandemic, owing creditors 3.5 billion euros and 1.9 billion euros had vanished from Wirecard's balance sheet. This resulted in the company's share price collapsing 98 percent and former CEO Markus Braun was arrested on suspicion of accounting fraud.

Wirecard AG was a new breed of Fintech company that supplied electronic payment transaction services, risk management, and dispensed physical and virtual credit cards. It was formed at the height of the dot-com bubble but by 2002, it was close to liquidating until Markus Braun injected his own capital and joined as CEO. He rationalized the company and focused on internet payment services for the adult and gambling websites. The company was listed on the Frankfurt Stock Exchange and part of the DAX stock index from September 2018 to August 2020. The company had been plagued by a series of investigative reports from the *Financial Times* into claims regarding. Accounting fraud at one point, the company had a market capitalization of 24 billion euros and just before it became insolvent, it was valued at 12 billion euros.

There was a major period of expansion, and Wirecard Asia Pacific was founded in Singapore in 2007. In 2008, Wirecard was highly innovative and introduced virtual prepaid credit cards for online payment and ironically in 2009 a fraud prevention suite for fraud detection. In 2014, Wirecard expanded into Oceania, Africa, and the Middle East. The 2016 acquisition of *Prepaid Card Services* from Citigroup gave the company a foothold into the Americas resulting in the same year a purchase of a South American internet payment service provider in Brazil. In 2019, SoftBank even invested in Wirecard and the company made its Chinese entry in 2019 with the acquisition of the Beijing-based *AllScore Payment Services*.

The expansion and acquisition masked the accounting fraud, which was fueling its duplicitous success. It later transpired that the company was utilizing the *round-tripping* scheme from its Singapore office to deceive its external auditors and record fictitious revenue. The scam was engineered by Edo Kurniawan, the former head of accounting for Asia-Pacific Operations, who instructed his colleagues in this nefarious technique where ;

> a lump of money would leave the bank Wirecard owns in Germany, show its face on the balance sheet of a dormant subsidiary in Hong Kong, depart to sit momentarily in the books of an external 'customer', then travel back to Wirecard in India, where it would look to local auditors like legitimate business revenue (**Financial Times 2019**).

The *Financial Times* in 2019 reported that profits at Wirecard Dubai and Dublin were falsely overstated; in fact, they comprised of fictitious sales. The grossly inflated revenue allowed Wirecard to even borrow 3.2 billion euros from banks and investors and gain a coveted bank license from the Hong Kong Monetary Authority to supply prepaid bank cards to consumers and organizations in China.

When it was officially discovered by EY that 1.9 billion euros had gone missing from the company escrow account, it hastened the end of Wirecard who quickly defaulted on its multibillion-euro loans and became Germany's biggest accounting scandal to date.

The accounting fraud, if not economic crimes perpetuated at Enron, WorldCom, Adelphia, Global Crossing, Parmalat S.p.A., Lehman Brothers, Toshiba, and Wirecard AG, all involved financial manipulation and falsification and were major corporate scandals. Although there are some similarities between these incidents, each example had its own unique traits and effects, the following is a brief yet insightful comparison:

Enron: Off-balance-sheet enterprises or special purpose vehicles were used by Enron to conceal debt and exaggerate earnings. Mark-to-market accounting was used to record anticipated in reality dubious future earnings in advance. Aggressive revenue recognition techniques, as well as the understating of revenues, expenses, and asset values, were used to manipulate the financial statements. This all caused Enron to fail, file for bankruptcy, and dissolve the doyen of the audit world Arthur Andersen, its external or statutory auditors.

WorldCom: This company inflated assets by inappropriate capitalization and overstated revenue and incorrectly classified operating costs as capital costs to boost earnings. This appeared to demonstrate superior financial performance but was a charade underpinned by false accounting entries. Consequently, World-Com filed for bankruptcy, which at the time was one of the biggest in American history.

Adelphia: The company's founders and executives, the Rigas family, were involved in the misuse of cash as they fraudulently borrowed money and illegally combined personal and business finances. Financial statements were misrepresented by concealing liabilities eventually Adelphia went bankrupt including the Rigas family members' criminal convictions.

Global Crossing: This organization used questionable accounting procedures to inflate revenue, utilized capacity swaps, and inflated assets to increase profits. The financial statements were fraudulently altered to give the impression that the company was financially sound; ultimately, the company became bankrupt and had to sell its assets to pay its creditors.

Parmalat S.p.A: To conceal debt and inflated assets, the company used false transactions and offshore corporations. Financial statements were manipulated by using fraudulent documents and inflated cash amounts with the support of banks and external auditors, that is, *A complete fraud.* Parmalat was forced to file for bankruptcy, making it one of the biggest corporate failures and scandals in European history.

Lehman Brothers: This once-renowned bank used creative accounting to tamper with its balance sheet and conceal risk. It used repo transactions improperly to hide debt and fictitiously boost financial ratios. Off-balance-sheet businesses were used to minimize leverage causing Lehman Brothers to go bankrupt and significantly contribute to the 2008 global financial crunch.

Toshiba: The company engaged in accounting irregularities that led to the overstatement of profits over several years. Financial statements were manipulated by failing to properly recognize future profits and delaying the acknowledgment of expenses resulting in overstated asset values and exorbitant sales. After a lengthy investigation, Toshiba was severely reprimanded by Japanese regulators and suffered a major correction in its stock price.

Wirecard AG: To give a false image of financial performance, the company fabricated its revenue, profits, and assets. This was achieved by planning and executing arrangements with third parties to erroneously overstate income again with the support of its auditors and company executives. Wirecard AG went bankrupt and highlighted serious regulatory and corporate governance flaws.

Whilst financial manipulation and misrepresentation were involved in all these accounting fraud case studies, the specific techniques used varied. Falsifying financial documents, exaggerating revenues, and assets, and hiding debt were recurring themes among them. It is interesting to note and suggested that external auditors colluded with senior management in the case of Enron, Parmalat, and Wirecard, which extended these frauds for years and brought disrepute to the audit profession. These scandals have had a huge impact on stakeholders including investors, employees, and the wider financial markets through bankruptcies, legal penalties, and other factors.

Thus far, it is apparent that accounting fraud occurs because of multiple factors, including greed and misinterpreting or aggressively applying accounting standards, all in a bid to maintain profitability and, ultimately, a stable and growing share price, which will be explored in the upcoming sections. It can be clearly seen that accounting fraud causes major damage to internal and external stakeholders such as investors, employees, and society at large.

Accounting fraud occurs in approximately 10 percent of internal fraud cases; however, the median cost of Accounting Fraud is $975 k in comparison with asset misappropriation, which has a median loss of $125 k in 83.5 percent of cases (ACFE 2016). It is suggested that major accounting scandals, for example, Enron, have increased the concerns of investors in accounting fraud. The chairman of the SEC commented in the aftermath of the global financial crunch that:

> One of the fundamental requirements for rational investing and efficient capital formation is the availability of high-quality information. One of our core functions is collecting and making publicly available financial and other relevant information from public companies. (Cited Jackson 2015, 6)

Hence, the well-being of financial markets is dependent on the production of robust financial information, that is, financial statements.

Synopsis of Accounting Fraud

Following notorious fraud scandals as outlined in previous sections, investors' concerns about fraud, in general, and accounting or financial statement fraud have risen. Hence, this section aims to provide an

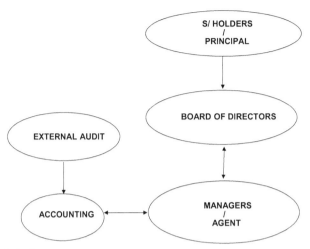

Figure 1.1 Corporate governance cosmos

outline of accounting fraud, including its nature, economic impact, types, and how it is perpetrated.

Sheikh (2017) created a useful framework to examine corporate governance salient to the study of accounting fraud, called the corporate governance cosmos; see Figure 1.1. He reminds us that the primary objective of a company is to maximize profits and therefore enhance the wealth of its shareholders. This is achieved by utilizing internally generated accounting information, which informs decision making. The important questions that arise during the potentially incongruent pursuit of profit and wealth maximization are who exercises responsibility and accountability, and what relationships and possible conflicts exist between *principals* and their *agents*, that is, **the agency problem**.

Shareholders are known as the *principals*, and the directors are the *agents*. It is contended that the extent to which boards of directors act in the interests of shareholders and in the execution of their fiduciary duties such as wealth maximization is dependent on which of the seven perspectives is taken on corporate social responsibility.

The seven positions vary from a minimalist perspective to the extreme, written from the stance that organizations need to move away from a purely profit motive to social and economic agendas. Their viewpoint emphasized trustworthy Corporate Social Reporting

(CSR), due to concerns of current CSR reporting lacking objectivity, for example, *greenwashing*, which is making fraudulent claims regarding the environmental credentials of products or the company itself. The following are the seven types:

- **Pristine Capitalists**: This viewpoint states that stakeholders view CSR as an obstacle to conducting business and stresses no responsibilities beyond that of shareholders and creditors. Though pristine capitalists accept there are social and environmental costs of undertaking business, they view this as a responsibility of society in general rather than that of organizations. On the other hand, such a position may tolerate governmental regulation that transforms social costs to real costs for use in maximizing profits.

- **Expedients** move slightly further than the pristine capitalists and consider CSR objectives if and only if contribute constructively to the economic interests of the organization. Expedients will take a long-term view that investing in CSR is beneficial for the bottom line, returning money to investors based on a robust reputation and sound public relations.

- **Supporters of social contracts** are organizations that acknowledge the concerns of external stakeholders affected by their decisions. This is achieved through contracts with those affected by decisions of the organization which are enforceable through a range of mechanisms.

- **Social ecologists** and social ecology can be considered as a paradigm shift in CSR, as organizations are considered the root of all environmental issues such pollution. Consequently, organizations must alter their approaches and consciously welcome CSR as the model going forward. This position contends that commercial enterprises and large organizations are primarily responsible for environmental destructions and therefore take the initiative in resolving environmental issues.

- **Socialists**: Organizations with a socialist ethos attempt to create an egalitarian equality within the organization and with all its vested social and economic interests. Hence, many socialists view the capitalism as exploitive and unstable, instead choosing to construct a society that shares the risk and reward equally.

- **Radical Feminists**: This stance has nothing to do with the women's movement. Rather, a radical feminist organization theoretically seeks to apply feminine values, such as cooperation in all organizational transactions. Since it is argued that business dealings are over-masculine in nature, leading to many social problems that can be resolved through feminine values.

- **Deep Ecologist**: The position of a deep ecologist argues that human beings are not superior to other living organisms and therefore do not have special rights or privileges over resources or life above those of any other sentient being. Deep ecologists will question the requirement for industry and commerce, instead fostering self-sufficiency and sustainability.

The groundbreaking study of Jensen and Meckling (1976) established that the principal–agent problem arises when a principal produces an environment in which an agent's incentives are incongruous with those of the principal. The burden is on the principal to create incentives or mechanisms for the agent to make certain that they behave as the principal desires, for example, to maximize shareholder wealth. This includes financial incentives to avoid information asymmetry such as overvalued equity. It is argued that managerial opportunism is a major determinant in these scandals, for example, managers who are remunerated for short-term results will potentially report misleading information, that is, accounting fraud, because short-term gains outweigh the long-term ones such as pension obligations. An extreme example of asymmetric information and agency cost is noted when an executive is aware of a takeover and secretly facilitates the sale of the company at a lower price by engineering a lower share price by releasing poor results to the market or convincing shareholders regarding the sale. Later, the executive is handsomely rewarded with a golden handshake or board position in the new company for managing the sale.

As noted earlier, accounting information is generated internally, and therefore the role of external audit is to dampen moral hazard and the abuse of asymmetric information by the agents, that is, accounting fraud. It is not the role of external auditors to detect fraud, but it is considered the norm that they have an active function in it. External audit promotes assurance and emphasizes trust in the financial information produced by companies. On the other hand, external auditors may be held liable if an accounting fraud case is not discovered and this phenomenon is known as the *audit expectations gap*. In view of a growing number of accounting fraud scandals, there is significant demand on the audit profession, by professional accountancy bodies, to improve audit quality and, by extension, accounting fraud detection. Despite this, research suggests that the external auditors are still deficient at assessing accounting fraud.

In recent years, the study of accounting fraud has grown significantly, and therefore the detection of financial fraud has become an ever more demanding and important task. Dorminey et al. (2012) argue that accounting fraud detection requires the collective work of "corporate governance professionals," namely, the board of directors, the audit committee, senior management, and internal and external auditors. It is suggested that understanding the various strands of accounting fraud should enable external auditors to better gauge the fraud risks inherent in an economic entity *However, this does not explain why* accounting fraud *continues.*

Woodcock (2015) suggests that in spite of the Sarbanes–Oxley Act of 2002, major improvements in internal controls, "Many Eyes Are on the Lookout for Fraud," including academics; analysts; and regulators incentivizing the reporting/whistleblowing of Accounting Fraud through the Frank–Dodds Act 2014, AF persists.

The Magnitude and Economic Consequences of Accounting Fraud

Accounting fraud occurs when financial reports materially misrepresent the information or when material facts are not fully disclosed in such reports. Accounting fraud has also been referred to as *management fraud* because it is probably undertaken by management for example in

Enron, where executives were charged with creating complex accounting schemes to make Enron look more profitable to facilitate personal gains. This has been acknowledged by International Standard on Auditing (ISA) No. 240, The Auditor's Responsibilities Relating to Fraud in an Audit of Financial Statements:

> Management is in a unique position to perpetrate fraud because of management's ability to manipulate accounting records and prepare fraudulent financial statements by overriding controls that otherwise appear to be operating effectively. Due to the unpredictable way in which such override could occur, it is regarded as a significant risk of material misstatement due to fraud (AICPA 2021, 240).

According to accounting researchers, accounting fraud involves deliberate omissions or nondisclosures in financial statements that are intended to mislead users of financial statements. Others argue that accounting fraud is the intentional attempt by companies to mislead users of financial statements by producing materially misstated company accounts.

It was discovered that the share price of a company fell steeply once it became public knowledge that it had engaged in accounting fraud, such as with the UK-listed company Tesco in 2017 that admitted that its 2014 profits were overstated by £250 million. It is acknowledged that the consequences of accounting fraud are far-reaching and can lead to the erosion of investors' confidence in the audit profession and the capital markets, damaging companies and forcing them to hire new talent, with overall harm to the economy and society.

Corporate governance is the method by which organizations are directed and controlled. Boards of directors are accountable for the governance of their companies by creating official and clear protocols for ensuring equitable financial reporting, coupled with strong risk management and internal control systems/culture. Shareholders engage with the directors and the auditors to ensure that a suitable governance model is established. It is maintained that the role of detecting and, above all, preventing fraud is in the remit of management and those charged with governance.

A weak internal control system coupled with poor governance could increase the likelihood of accounting fraud, which is supported by the global 2018 ACFE fraud study. This also highlighted another significant factor, *ineffective board leadership*, which could increase the risk of fraud. Several studies have established a positive correlation between poor corporate governance and accounting fraud. It was discovered that the risk of accounting fraud dampens when there are more external directors on the board with vested interests in the company. Accounting fraud is more likely to happen when power remains solely in the hands of insiders because they have access to asymmetric information, which informs decision making.

According to ISA 240 (The Auditors Responsibility Relating to Fraud in an Audit of Financial Statements) (AICPA 2021), external auditors have several objectives in relation to fraud:

a. To identify and assess the risks of material misstatement of the financial statements due to fraud.

b. To obtain enough appropriate audit evidence regarding the assessed risks of material misstatement due to fraud, through designing and implementing appropriate responses.

c. To respond appropriately to fraud or suspected fraud identified during the audit.

ISA 240 also requires external auditors to assess and respond to the risk of accounting fraud and to categorize that risk into three categories: risk of motives/pressure to commit fraud, risk of opportunity to commit fraud, and risk of rationalization of fraud (187:A125), that is, the fraud triangle, which will be shortly discussed.

External auditors may be held liable if companies unexpectedly go out of business or if it is found that important personnel are involved in fraud. However, it is important to acknowledge that there is an *audit expectations gap,* which is defined as the gap between what the society expects from external auditors and what it gains, although ISAs supply little guidance to external auditors with respect to the risk assessment of fraud. They can act as a valuable buffer against fraud because most fraudsters are afraid of being exposed and of the related penalties. An important study established the link between audit committee features and the consistency of financial reporting. The study also found that the risk of accounting fraud reporting is negatively correlated with audit committee independence and frequency of audit committee meetings, that is, the latter mechanism deters accounting fraud.

It is argued that the audit expectation gap can be reduced by enhancing fraud risk assessment and employing better fraud detection methods. ISA 240 insists that external auditors utilize professional skepticism or doubt while ascertaining the risk of fraud. On the other hand, it is believed that professional doubt is not enough and that the external auditors need to use *critical thinking*,' which necessitates an appreciation of the motivations behind accounting fraud. This leads into the next section, where the author will examine the key motivations, theories, and approaches behind the phenomenon of accounting fraud.

The Drivers of Accounting Fraud

The literature concerning the motivations for management to perpetrate accounting fraud concentrates mainly on pay, attracting and/or maintaining finance, exceeding or upholding market expectations, covering up financial problems, or socioeconomic and psychological pressures. The authors will now explore each, in turn beginning with *pay*.

Pay

Senior management remuneration contracts usually cover all or a mixture of share options, cash compensation, including bonuses, and share ownership. Share options allow holders to purchase company shares at an option exercise price that may be, but is not always, below the stock market price. An investigation of recent accounting scandals concluded that the major factor in such unprecedented frauds was exaggerated management compensation. It is argued that executives' pay that is based on options tends to engage in higher risk. It was discovered that senior management of publicly listed companies such as AIG were highly remunerated but made poor judgments, and, in some instances, there was alleged accounting fraud. It is suggested that management can be under immense pressure, especially when company success is directly correlated with their compensation plan, which can make them select accounting policies that may result in accounting fraud. This has also been noted by regulators such as the **Financial Services Authority (2009)**, who observed that executive pay contracts in British banks can encourage some managers to take unjustified risks that apparently, in the short term, generated exorbitant windfalls but eventually jeopardized the entire banking system. Further academic studies have found that pay contracts could engender short termism including profit growth, a high share price, and, ultimately, a higher stock-option value at the expense of shareholder wealth. Hence, it is maintained when bona fide results no longer support the share price, some managers will resort to accounting misapplication and fraud to maintain the façade of short-term profit growth and stock and option values.

Even where cash is the major constituent of the pay contract, this may still not guarantee or lessen accounting fraud if there is a culture of corruption and management is not concerned with shareholder welfare.

According to agency theory, increasing company ownership should diminish a manager's desire to engage in accounting fraud. Therefore, equity-based compensation has become a favored technique to reduce the gap between management and shareholders and expand the value of the company. However, recent frauds, including Enron and post-Enron, have been executed by managers who had material ownership of the company. A sophisticated model was used to investigate managers' equity-based remuneration contracts and discovered that managers will usually deceive the company earlier with stock options rather than with a comparable cash pay package consisting of shares.

In contrast, it has been reported that higher ownership or equity-based remuneration will not necessarily reduce the propensity to undertake fraud unless the advantage from fraud is completely mitigated via the penalty. Therefore, more managers may engage in a strategy to behave fraudulently when it suits them. An empirical study, investigating the link between incentive-based remuneration packages and the probability of accounting fraud, established that managers of companies with weak operating performance or results usually commit accounting fraud and have equity-based pay structures. It is suggested that remunerating nonexecutive directors in the UK context with stock options may weaken their independent oversight and potentially motivate them to misstate financial results.

The Requirement to Obtain Finance

Research suggests that the need to obtain finance can be a trigger for senior management to execute accounting fraud. For example, there may be a need to raise more capital or alternative lines of credit, and accounting fraud may be the only mechanism to achieve these financial goals.

A pre-Enron study established that the key determinant of accounting fraud was the requirement to raise further capital. The need for cheap external finance, coupled with the requirement to sidestep debt covenant limits, can induce management to maliciously influence earnings. Certain analysts hold that the need to secure higher cash amounts when issuing fresh stock/shares can be a purported reason for management to commit accounting fraud. It is argued that senior management may encounter intense pressure to continuously issue suitable results; otherwise, external stakeholders may lose confidence or jeopardize access to additional capital. It has been suggested that pending long-term finance, including debt or equity, maybe a motive for companies to engage in accounting fraud. It is also believed that if management wants to issue equity at a reasonable cost, they may be more inclined to engage in earnings management.

Beating Market Expectations

Previous literature indicates that exceeding or maintaining market expectations can potentially motivate management to undertake accounting fraud. For example, it may desire long-term finance from an initial public offering (IPO), achieve corporate objectives, or beat market analysts. It is argued that senior management is aware that not maintaining analysts' forecasts can have a detrimental effect on company share price performance and that thus there is pressure on it to alter earnings through accounting fraud. It was reported that listed companies are under intense pressure to issue earnings reports that, at a minimum, meet market expectations rather than maximizing shareholder wealth because senior pay would be jeopardized.

The Cooks, Recipes, Incentives, Monitoring, End Results (C R I M E) model created by Rezaee (2005) established that incentives for accounting fraud included upholding market expectations by exaggerating the company results, raising additional cash through an IPO, achieving corporate objectives, and manipulating share prices to raise the demand for issuance of more share capital. On the other hand, it is contended by Albrecht et al. (2008) that it is improbable, if not unrealistic, for Wall Street expectations to encourage senior management to execute accounting fraud. However, it is contended that the desire to meet outside earnings targets causes accounting fraud, especially in the short term. Perols and Lougee (2010) argued that "meet or beat analyst forecasts" are probably forcing companies to commit accounting fraud even when there is no evidence of previous earnings management or accounting fraud.

C R I M E L

One of the authors (Faisal Sheikh) extended the original C R I M E model to include L—learning, that is, what is the key learning that we can take away so that we avoid the scourge of accounting fraud?

The author analyzed 33 case studies/companies discussed in the important **ACFE-sponsored book, Wells (2011)**, which was edited by the seasoned and well-respected fraud investigator and commentator, Joseph T. Wells. The industry, whether the CEO and/or the CFO, were involved and if they possessed any psychopathic tendencies, were also highlighted by the author.

The 33 case studies are comprised of a variety of industries, ranging from bioscience to transport, 21 percent of which are concentrated in financial services. Twenty of the case studies are American, and the remainder are international, underscoring the global phenomenon of accounting fraud covering the following countries: Austria, Cyprus, Hong Kong, India, Japan, Jersey, Kenya, Malaysia (two), Saudi Arabia, Spain, UAE, and Venezuela.

It was noted that 82 percent of *cooks*/**perpetrators** were male and the balance female, suggesting that this is a male-dominated crime. A surprising 94 percent of the offenders demonstrated psychopathic tendencies, such as a charismatic personality, coupled with a desire for absolute control and manipulation. This potentially suggests that global top management is unbalanced and ruthless, which fits the image of the character of the financial fraudster, Gordon Gekko, as played by Michael Douglas in the acclaimed movie *Wall Street*. It is also evident that in a significant number of cases, 42 percent, there was collusion between the CEO and the CFO, suggesting that governance is a real problem, when there is a well-articulated and functioning control environment because it is subject to management override.

The most favored *recipes*/**methods** of executing the accounting fraud were illegal earnings management, 58 percent, and increasing the value of assets, 33 percent. Illegitimately reducing expenses and liabilities was also utilized. The major *incentive* for committing AF was greed, which occurred because of leading a lavish lifestyle.

It was established that the ***incentives*** for committing accounting fraud were breaching debt covenants, gaining new lines of credit, and meeting market expectations supported the literature. There were other less-known but important motivating factors, such as pressure from the parent company, sale of the business, and a company embarking on an IPO or listing on a public stock exchange such as the New York Stock Exchange (NYSE).

It was noted that ***monitoring*** becomes redundant where management override is possible, which was present in 45 percent of the case studies. This supports the adage that a *fish rots from the head down,* meaning that a corrupt senior leadership is the root cause of an organization's failure and demise caused by accounting fraud. Senior leadership sets the tone and culture for an organization; thus, in 33 percent of the cases, there was a poor control culture or willfully poor internal controls. There were several cases showing examples of *control fraud*, where the CEO, the CFO, and internal and external auditors all colluded to execute the accounting fraud. In this rare phenomenon, it is practically impossible to detect the fraud until the company implodes. The only solution to detecting and fighting accounting fraud is an anonymous whistle-blower hotline. It was also found, in several cases, that external auditors were negligent probably because of poor training or knowledge of the client or industry, which underscores the importance of a quality external audit, although it is not the job of the external auditor to actively search for accounting fraud.

Surprisingly, the **end results of** *Accounting Fraud* only resulted in 33 percent of perpetrators going to prison, suggesting that white-collar criminals are not perceived as being as dangerous as other types of criminals. However, as discussed in the section regarding "The Significance and Cost of Accounting Fraud," the socioeconomic costs of accounting fraud are significant and ultimately destroy trust in the capital markets. On the other hand, forensic accountants and fraud examiners require knowledge of accounting, auditing, and investigative skills to conduct an examination of the finances of an individual or business to unearth and crucially prove the existence of accounting fraud. Therefore, it is not uncommon for regulators to fine and disbar convicted CFOs from practicing again, as occurred in 15 percent of the sample. In as many as 27 percent of cases, once the crime had been discovered, it was dealt with internally, probably to avoid the reputational damage and the negative impact on external stakeholders such as lenders and investors. This course of action is problematic in that it will not lead to a root and branch clean-up of the culture and implicitly signals that accounting fraud will be tolerated. In some extreme cases, even when the fraud was detected, nothing happened to the criminals, and they were left free to wreak havoc in their next company. Ultimately, accounting fraud is synonymous with corporate failure, as in the notorious case of Enron, and 15 percent of companies studied liquidated after the discovery of the accounting fraud. This can also be viewed as an opportunity for the company to change, as 85 percent of the companies survived and may even have flourished.

The author believes that accounting fraud is a classic case of agency conflict and moral hazard where inappropriate incentivization, such as excessive bonuses or stock options, perpetuates a culture of short termism, where the line between *profit making* and *profit taking* becomes very blurred. Hence, in the author's study of 33 international companies, the key strategic learning themes gauged were around culture, control environment, and the role of the auditor, as summarized in Table 1.1.

Covering Up Company Financial Problems

According to an in-depth study involving 200 companies' senior management, many have undertaken accounting fraud to improve declining results, maintain or increase share prices, avoid delisting, or conceal the fact that company assets were stolen or utilized for personal use. The companies in the study were either experiencing material losses or were close to breakeven, which suggests that poor company results may incentivize accounting fraud.

It has been noted that companies experiencing severe financial distress were more likely to commit accounting fraud and that, consequently, external auditors should remain vigilant. This pattern has also been noted in bankrupt firms that may be more prone to undertake accounting fraud to cover up financial problems and engage in aggressive earnings management before company failure. After studying the most notorious accounting scandals of the early 2000s, such as Enron, researchers concluded that the most important motivator to commit accounting fraud was growing debt and the need to conceal it. Further research suggests that senior management who commit accounting fraud are usually attempting to avoid major corrections to the company share price. A multiple regression model using a sample of Malaysian companies in 2008 to ascertain the drivers of accounting fraud found that severe financial problems were the primary variable. A study of fraudulent financial statements by listed Chinese companies,

Table 1.1 Key themes from C R I M E L model

Culture—1	• An ethical culture must be set at the top
	• Long tenure and a position of trust does not clear some of suspicion
	• CFOs/CEOs with psychopathic tendencies cannot be treated and need to be removed sooner rather than later, or else the long-term viability of the organization is under serious threat
	• Growing or stable dividends are not a signal of a well-run company
	• Investors should not be impressed by glossy brochures and the "elder statesman"
Culture—2	• Audit committees and the internal audit function must be completely independent
	• Changes in the lifestyle of senior management or junior staff should be considered a potential red flag
	• "Control fraud" can and does occur; hence, boards should consider fintech solutions such as blockchain systems that make fraud next to impossible as any changes can be viewed by all participants in the ecosystem
	• Simple HR checks can prevent the hiring of incompetent staff, including at senior level
Control environment	• There must be a robust system of internal controls to prevent Accounting Fraud, although these will always be at the mercy of management override
	• Wherever economically feasible, there must be a segregation of duties and never too much reliance on one employee, which can be dampened through job rotation, and there should be insistence on the taking of annual leave
	• Board members should be wary of complex structures
	• An anonymous whistle-blower hotline is a cheap and highly effective tool to detect and deter Accounting Fraud

(Continued)

Table 1.1 (Continued)

Role of the External Auditor	• The auditor must always remain skeptical and err on the side of caution
	• Auditors must keep "management representations" to a minimum
	• Auditors should be knowledgeable about the client and the industry, including KPIs, and thoroughly critique "people, processes, and procedures"
	• The auditors must undertake in-depth analytical reviews to ascertain any anomalies
	• Although it is not the role of the auditor to discover A, they should be well versed in forensic accounting techniques, look for patterns or anomalies such as in revenue, and fully understand why journals are prepared

using multiple regression analysis, showed that companies used earning management techniques to conceal losses to avoid being delisted from the stock exchange. In the Egyptian context, it was found that the senior management's need to maintain, if not exceed, previous financial results was the major motivation to engage in accounting fraud.

Socioeconomic Challenges

Researchers agree that personality type is a significant factor that plays a major role in the fraudster profile. For example, a passive person is less likely to engage in fraud than an active person. A research study suggests that executives are motivated to engage in accounting fraud for the following reasons: excessive may be an extreme association with the business, a huge ego, familial pressures, company expansion strategies, and concern for company existence. A groundbreaking study adopting a multidisciplinary approach to their study utilizing the lens of criminology, economics, psychology and sociology, economics, and criminology to establish the likelihood of. They found *socio-level* factors such as differential association and strain, *industry-level factors* such as culture and values, and *firm-level factors* such as board structure that had an impact on the likelihood of accounting fraud.

Undoubtedly, greed is an important motive for undertaking accounting fraud. An interesting study established that executives whose identity is constructed around the company are prone to commit accounting fraud on account of poor results as a *protective mechanism*. Notions of *self-esteem* can also encourage senior management to engage in accounting fraud. **Psychological factors, including the dark triad, will be elaborated by the authors in the next chapter.**

Chapter 2 will briefly discuss the types of accounting fraud techniques mentioned in the literature and introduce the original model, namely, the fraud triangle that purports to explain fraud in general which can also be applied to accounting fraud. This model will be critiqued and extended to incorporate an element of the *dark triad* (narcissism, Machiavellianism, and psychopathy), namely, **psychopathy**.

CHAPTER 2

The Fraud Triangle and How to Discern Accounting Fraud

The Fraud Triangle: Even the Most Complicated Things Can be Simple.
—Pete Miller, Shareholder in the audit and assurance practice at the accounting firm Clark Nuber PS, headquartered in Bellevue, Washington

We begin this chapter by exploring and critiquing the foremost model present in the white-collar crime literature namely, the fraud triangle. We will also examine alternative models that can help explain accounting fraud. The prevention, deterrence, and detection of accounting fraud will also be briefly examined. Finally, we will probe the psychology literature specifically the dark triad to better understand accounting fraud **which will help to model the corporate psychopath accountant.**

Fraud Model

The most famous model claiming to explain fraud in general and specifically accounting fraud is the fraud triangle. Over the years, accounting researchers have updated the fraud triangle, resulting in extended models that appear to better understand the nature of fraud.

The three constituents of the fraud triangle (pressure, opportunity, rationalization) have been successfully integrated by important regulators and professional bodies in the United States, where it is the bedrock of the **following:**

- Association of Certified Fraud Examiners' (ACFE) *Fraud Examiners Manual*
- Public Company Accounting Oversight Boards' (PCAOB) AU Section 316, *Consideration of Fraud in a Financial Statement Audit*
- American Institute of Certified Public Accountants' (AICPA) SAS no. 99, *Consideration of Fraud in a Financial Statement Audit*

This chapter will outline and evaluate the fraud triangle and discuss whether the dark triad can help better explain, detect, and prevent accounting fraud.

The Fraud Triangle

It is an interesting fact that Donald Cressey was a student of Sutherland and began his research in 1950 when he was exploring "criminal violation of financial trust." Cressey interviewed 250 prisoners over five months in the state of Illinois who fulfilled two criteria: (a) the person had accepted a position of trust and (b) the same person went on to violate this trust and undertake a crime (Cressey 1950, 1953). He was attempting to develop a general theory of criminal behavior, which resulted from the violation of financial trust that occurred because of learned behavior during the normal course of business or professional activities, or the misdemeanors that resulted during business or professional activities and had not been learned. This was rejected because social learning did not appear to explain the crimes. Furthermore, many of the prisoners stated that they knew what they were doing was unlawful and incorrect. Moreover, they explained that they had operated in isolation and did not know anybody else who had committed such crimes in their business or profession. Cressey adapted the original hypothesis and concluded that three factors were necessary for the criminal violation of trust to take place: (a) a *nonshareable* financial difficulty, (b) an acknowledgment that the problem could be resolved by violating trust, and (c) the capacity to verbalize or later rationalize the criminal act. This hypothesis later developed into the fraud triangle, namely *pressure*, *opportunity*, and *rationalization*.

Pressure

Cressey originally limited the pressure side of the triangle to a nonshareable financial problem because, he argued, individuals in positions of financial trust also had an obligation to avoid gambling, excessive drinking, and having extramarital affairs in consideration of their social position. However, when these people began indulging in illicit activities, they would start piling up debts, which must be kept secret and, consequently, became a nonshareable financial problem. Rather than seeking help, these individuals violate their trusted positions and commit fraud. **Cressey** went on to refine and extend the nonshareable financial problem into six groups: (a) *violation of an assigned responsibility*, (b) *problems stemming from personal setbacks*, (c) *problems arising from business failures*, (d) *problems resulting from loneliness*, (e) *problems caused by an incessant desire to achieve high social status, and, finally*, (f) *problems resulting from poor employee–employer interactions*.

Regarding a violation of an assigned responsibility, Cressey observed that trusted individuals believed that they had to maintain a certain standard and uphold a high reputation in their social and professional gatherings. When they start engaging in illicit activities such as gambling, they do not seek help because they fear losing their social status and their trusted position, that is, suffering from a vice. Second, problems stemming from personal setbacks become nonshareable because people in trusted positions believe that they will lose credibility even though they are aware that other associates could help them, that is, poor judgment. Third, business failure can be genuine, but it becomes a nonshareable problem that they must resolve themselves, even in an illegal manner. Fourth, alienation breeds nonshareable problems because people cannot turn to a support network, such as friends, to help resolve the issue. Thus far, the problems have been about maintaining status, but an incessant desire to achieve a higher status usually occurs as individuals start living beyond their means, creating a nonshareable problem that must be financed by utilizing fraudulent methods. In the final problem, although the person is in a trusted position, they may resent their employer because they feel underpaid, overworked, or not properly treated; however, they believe they must carry on working. This becomes a nonshareable problem because they cannot share their dissatisfaction with other colleagues, fearing they will lose their trusted position. The problems, individually or collectively, may lead a person to violate their trusted position and seek payback from their company. **Lister (2007, 63)** defined pressure as the "source of heat for the fire."

All the pressure variables result from a *nonshareable* problem by people in a position of financial trust. However, as will be demonstrated later, when the theory was applied to other scenarios or positions, Cressey's understanding of pressure was flawed, and other factors could cause fraudulent behavior, such as an interesting typology by **Kassem and Higson (2012)**, Figure 2.1.

Opportunity

The second side of the triangle is the opportunity to violate trust. Initially, when the position of trust is obtained, the individual may not perceive any opportunity; however, once the *nonshareable* problem becomes apparent, the trusted person will begin to recognize that there is an opportunity for a resolution, albeit fraudulently. Cressey argued

Figure 2.1 Typology of pressure

Source: Adapted by authors.

that this shift in perception was based on experience and sources such as associates who engage in fraud or news stories. In addition, these trust violators need to possess the requisite skills and aptitude to commit and hide their fraudulent behavior. **It has been claimed** that the skill set that allows the trust violators to be hired is the same skill set that can be used to commit the fraud. ***Thus, a classic example is auditors or accountants who are trained to identify and remedy fraud, but when encountering a "nonshareable" problem they use their knowledge to take advantage of the control system, that is, a loophole, and hide their fraudulent actions.*** **Lister** considered that opportunity as the "fuel that keeps the fire going" and that even if a fraudster had a motive, they could not undertake a fraud without opportunity.

In short, opportunity is the view or perception held by fraudsters that (a) trust violations can solve their financial problem, (b) a control weakness has been identified, and (c) the probability of their violation being discovered is low.

Rationalization

The third side of the fraud triangle is characterized as rationalization, which is the trust violator's effort to dampen the inner conflict that occurs. This rationalization allows the fraudster to give expressions such as "I am borrowing not stealing" or "All people steal when they get into a tight spot" (**Cressey 1953**) to their deed, thus allowing them to maneuver internally between the contradiction of the trusted person and abuse of that trust, to resolve their nonshareable problem. According to theorists, rationalization allows fraudsters to justify their misdemeanors and stay within their comfort zone. Many of the fraudsters acknowledged that they were committing a crime but denied any wrongdoing, enabling them to preserve their self-respect. Also, many were first-time offenders who believed that they were honest and had got themselves entangled in a problem.

Researchers argue that rationalization can be further divided into denial of (a) responsibility, (b) injury, and (c) victimization. A denial of responsibility is the fraudsters' justification that they are left with no options and that, consequently, blame is transferred to the victims, or denial of any personal benefit, making their fraudulent acts selfless. A denial of injury implies that the harm resulting from their trust violation will not hurt anyone, including people in big organizations, or if they are insured, that is, moral hazard. Finally, denial of victimization occurs when the fraudsters believe that their victims deserve what they are getting or that their revenge is fully justified. The final type of denial is prevalent in toxic workplaces, and a study highlighted that it was easier for employees to rationalize theft from disagreeable work environments. **Lister** defined rationalization as "oxygen that keeps the fire burning."

Thus far, the constituents of the fraud triangle have been discussed, namely pressure, opportunity, and rationalization, which can be shown in Figure 2.2.

In 2002, the AICPA incorporated the constituents of the fraud triangle into Statement on Auditing Standards 99:

Three conditions generally are present when fraud occurs. First, management or other employees have an incentive or are under pressure, which provides a reason to commit fraud. Second,

Figure 2.2 The fraud triangle

Source: Adapted by authors.

circumstances exist … that provide for a fraud to be perpetrated. Third, those involved are able to rationalize committing a fraudulent act (**AICPA 2021; AU 316.07**).

In 2009, the International Auditing and Assurance Standards Board issued an updated version of International Standard on Auditing 240 (ISA 240), which advised that external auditors consider the following three fraud risk factors: pressure to commit accounting fraud, which may exist when management is under pressure from external factors to achieve potentially unrealistic earnings; a key individual may exist who is in a position of trust or has knowledge of internal control deficiencies; and, finally, there may exist a culture that allows for the facilitation and therefore rationalization of fraud. The fraud triangle underpins the work of the ACFE.

Appraisal of the Fraud Triangle

The authors will now examine the literature that supports the fraud triangle. **A model was** developed that assessed the probability of significant accounting fraud or management fraud. Their model confirms that for fraud to take place it requires three important variables: motive, "a weak system or opportunity," and fraudsters who can rationalize their actions. According to this model, if any of the latter conditions are missing, it is improbable that accounting fraud will take place. A logistic regression model was created that predicted the frequency of fraud that supported all three conditions of the fraud triangle. This was validated by another academic, who found fraud triangle conditions in his sample of fraudulent companies. A robust, 2006, fraud prediction model, based on fraud triangle conditions, correctly classified fraud and nonfraud approximately 70 percent of the time. The model incorporated factors that were substitutes for pressure, opportunity, and rationalization. An interesting conceptual study argued that corporate fraud could be better understood by combining the constituents of the American Dream Theory (excessive focus on monetary success, exploitation of regulatory protocols, and the rationalization of fraudulent behavior) and the fraud triangle (pressure, opportunity, and rationalization).

An important study analyzed the major accounting scandals utilizing the lens of the fraud triangle of the past 10 years, concluding that greed, opportunities such as aggressive applications of GAAP, and, third, rationalization such as a lack of ethics education were the major reasons for such major accounting fraud. A study of four major South Korean conglomerates found that they were vulnerable to fraud as per the fraud triangle variables of pressure, opportunity, and rationalization.

Before critiquing the individual constituents of the fraud triangle, a notable problem with the model is whether it is a general theory of financial crime because it originally studied embezzlers. It is maintained by some analysts that the fraud triangle is a *framework* rather than a *fraud theory* and that there is therefore no fraud theory.

Apparently, **Albrecht (2014a)** coined the phrase *fraud triangle*, in 1991, when he and his team of researchers conducted a 1979 study in which they generalized Cressey's original model to relate to all types of fraud. **Morales et al. (2014)** contacted the ACFE who confirmed that "Dr. Cressey developed the three items (incentive, opportunity, and rationalization), but he did not call it the Fraud Triangle" (cited Huber 2016). It is suggested that Cressey agreed to the promotion of the *fraud triangle* because it was constructed on his work, and the founder of the ACFE, Dr. Wells, required Cressey's tacit endorsement for the creation of ACFE. **Lokanan (2015, 202)** states that "the fraud triangle endorses a body of knowledge that lacks the objective criteria required to adequately address every occurrence of fraud." He suggested that "[t]he ACFE's discourse conceptualizes fraud as a dishonest act perpetuated by an individual for personal enrichment," thus ignoring other influences. He further states that ACFE "perpetuates a discourse that presents a restricted version of fraud. Fraud is a multifaceted phenomenon, whose contextual factors may not fit into a framework. Consequently, the fraud triangle should not be taken as a sufficiently reliable model for anti-fraud professionals."

It has been highlighted that the fraud triangle is equilateral, implying that each side carries equal credence, but this has not been established to date. Some researchers argue that the fraud triangle is *U.S.-centric* and that until it incorporates societal-level factors such as culture it will remain deficient.

Rationalization has received little attention and may not *even be observable*, and, third, the fraud triangle is based on a single criminal, whereas recent frauds such as Enron were executed by multiple actors and that collusion is an important factor in fraud. An in-depth and critical study on a genealogy of the fraud triangle states that it lacks a sound explanation for collusive fraud and has become a professional tool for the ACFE at the expense of *micro-sociological* and *macro-sociological* theories of financial crime. It is argued that the fraud triangle ignores group dynamics and other nonfinancial motives such as greed and revenge. A comprehensive study of 1,500 executives concluded that "keeping up with the Joneses" was a major motive for fraud. Therefore, nonshareable information is not enough to trigger fraudulent behavior.

Beginning with the pressure side, many researchers have argued whether a nonshareable problem is even a necessary facet of fraud and whether theft can be explained by a need for further money. On the opportunity side, it is stated that other nonfinancial variables need to be considered, such as ego and ideology, that force fraudsters to undertake their crimes. It has also been argued that Cressey's model does not consider whether the trust violator has the capability that is necessary to undertake and conceal the fraud. It is suggested that the opportunity to undertake fraud is prevalent in firms that lack a strong corporate governance structure. It is argued that rationalization is difficult to discern and report and suggested that it should be replaced by *personal integrity*, which is easier to study.

Cohen et al. (2010) combined the fraud triangle and the theory of planned behavior, which highlighted personality traits as key fraud risk factors. Their study of words linked with rationalization was found to be more prevalent in fraudulent firms in contrast to a sample of control firms. A model was created that expanded the rationalization side of the fraud triangle to incorporate three psychological routes to fraud, namely, poor consciousness, perception in conjunction with rationalization, and thinking.

Collectively, these criticisms have led to extensions and updates of the original fraud triangle, which will now be examined.

The Triangle of Fraud Action

The triangle of fraud action, also known as the elements of fraud, in contrast to the fraud triangle, concentrates on the actions of a fraudster rather than the conditions under which fraud occurs. The triangle of fraud action differentiates between the white-collar criminal (whose actions are illustrated by the fraud triangle) and the white-collar crime. Rather than opportunity, pressure, and rationalization, the triangle of fraud action comprises the following observable components, namely, concealment, conversion, and the act.

Concealment is the effort expended to hide the fraudulent act such as *cooking the books* or shredding documentation. *Conversion* is the method utilized by the criminal to legitimize the fraud, such as overstating receivables to maximize revenue or money laundering. The *act* is the technique used by the perpetrator to commit the fraud, such as accounting fraud. The triangle of fraud action emphasizes the weak areas in the business rather than the conditions necessary to induce the fraudster. Therefore, it is a useful tool in preventing, detecting, and deterring fraud and consequently makes it difficult for the fraudster to deny the act. It is stated that since all three elements are observable, it is a more robust model of fraud than the fraud triangle.

The Fraud Scale

The fraud scale was created after a study showed that the fraud triangle was a poor predictor of fraud and that it was difficult to profile fraudsters. The fraud scale eliminates the rationalization element of the fraud triangle and replaces it with personal integrity.

The three features of the fraud scale can be modified to assess the probability of the fraud taking place. The scale has two arms: the left arm accommodates great opportunity and low personal integrity and the right arm has low pressure, lesser opportunity, and high personal integrity. It is argued that if the scale, Figure 2.3, moves to the left, there

Figure 2.3 The fraud scale

Source: Adapted by authors

is a greater probability of fraud occurring because these conditions result in a higher fraud risk, and the opposite is true if the scale tilts to the right. Consequently, if someone has a low level of personal integrity, both the probability of rationalization and fraud risk will increase.

MICE

Cressey (1950, 1953) argued that a nonshareable problem was the trigger for fraudulent behavior. However, recent major accounting scandals have demonstrated that fraudsters do not need nonshareable problems to undertake fraud. Hence, senior employees who have been convicted of fraud did not suffer from nonshareable problems such as a gambling addiction. It is argued that the major driver of fraud was a high self-image coupled with a competitive culture. Therefore, social status can pressure an executive to engage in white-collar crime when there is no apparent financial issue.

These observations led to the creation of the MICE, which amplifies the pressure side of the fraud triangle. The MICE variables are motivators to commit fraud: M stands for the pressure of money, I is for ideology, C represents coercion, and E is ego or entitlement. The model is considered a framework that can be utilized to understand the motives of fraudsters.

Figure 2.4 The fraud diamond
Source: Adapted by authors

The Fraud Diamond

The fraud diamond extended the fraud triangle by adding another element, namely, *capability of a fraudster*, see Figure 2.4, which plays a major role in the execution of fraud even if pressure, opportunity, and rationalization are present. Wolfe and Hermanson (2004) argue that the *capability* is the most important factor when a fraud is committed because the fraudster has discovered the opportunity to commit the fraud and is convinced that they possess the necessary skills and attitude to successfully execute it.

It is argued that the six features of a *capable fraudster* are as follows: the person, firstly, has an important position, second, the intellectual equipment to undertake the fraud, third, the requisite confidence, fourth, the ability to intimidate actors to help them undertake the fraud, fifth, the ability to habitually lie in order to maintain their position, and, finally, resistance to significant levels of stress because fraud can be a complex and drawn-out affair.

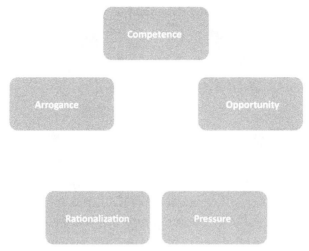

Figure 2.5 The fraud pentagon

Source: Adapted by authors

The Fraud Pentagon

The fraud diamond was further extended by including *arrogance and competence/capability*, resulting in the **Crowe Horwath Fraud Pentagon, see Figure 2.5. Marks (2009)** reasoned that the current business environment in comparison with that of the 1950s has changed significantly. The most notable changes are that corporations are multinational, engage more readily with outsourcing inputs, and employees are subject to performance-based compensation. This creates more pressure on employees, resulting in arrogance or lack of conscience and, consequently, a lack of accountability. Competence is the ability to undertake a fraudulent act by overriding internal and social protocols.

New Fraud Triangle Model

Kassem and Higson (2012) argued that as many factors as possible should be considered when a practitioner such as an auditor is attempting to understand accounting fraud. They proposed the amalgamation of several established fraud models, creating the new fraud triangle model (NFTM):

Fraud Triangle + Fraud Diamond + Fraud Scale + MICE Model = NFTM

The NFTM incorporates the attributes of *motivation, opportunity, integrity, and capability of the would-be fraudster.*

The A-B-C Model

The A-B-C model was proposed by **Ramamoorti et al. (2009)** and does not extend the fraud triangle. Instead, it focuses on the probability of the fraud under specific circumstances. The A-B-C model is made up of the following: *bad apples or an individual fraudster, bad bushels or collusive fraud, and bad crop or cultural and societal values that can affect the frequency of fraud.*

Predator Versus Accidental Fraudsters

It was discovered that 75 percent of fraud was committed by individuals who were usually honest, law-abiding, and who, in normal situations, would never attempt to commit a crime, that is, *the accidental fraudster.* This type of fraudster fits the fraud triangle. However, some people are predators who continuously break the law, and research suggests that after a first-time offense, rationalization becomes much easier, because the perpetrator becomes desensitized and will continue defrauding until apprehended. Therefore, for the predator, the fraud triangle collapses into opportunity, while pressure and rationalization change into arrogance, and the fraudulent act transforms into a whim or desire. It is believed that predators are well-organized and able to mislead auditors with their complex scheming.

The C R I M E Model

The C R I M E model is a fraud model developed by **Rezaee (2005),** where *cooks, recipes, incentives, monitoring, and end results* explain the causes and effects of accounting fraud. It highlights the importance of corporate governance and provides novel strategies to prevent accounting fraud. The *cooks* are the perpetrators of accounting fraud, and it was found that in 80 percent of cases either the CFO or CEO was responsible. The *recipes* were the techniques used to execute accounting fraud, and earnings management was the most popular method. The *incentives* were the motivations for committing accounting fraud and are usually understood to be economic but can also encompass psychological and ideological factors. The foremost *monitoring* mechanism is corporate governance. The *end results* of accounting fraud can be substantial, such as company liquidation and delisting from a capital market. The C R I M E model investigated nine cases that resulted in more than $500 billion of damage.

Nijenhuis (2016) extended the C R I M E framework by adding *S, which stands for sentences,* which were the legal sentences that the fraudsters received, including jail time or fines or community service that may prevent fraud.

Before we examine psychological factors that may cause accounting fraud, we need to briefly consider the prevention, deterrence, and detection.

Prevention, Deterrence, and Detection

Prevention and deterrence protocols are designed to lessen the opportunity for fraudsters, while detection occurs postfraud. It has been argued that when an organization has robust mandates, this sends strong signals to potential internal and external fraudsters. According to **Dorminey et al. (2012, 573),** fraud deterrence works when "(1) the perception of deterrence is present and (2) potential perpetrators recognize that they will be punished when caught."

It is contended that potential fraudsters must believe that detection is highly probable; otherwise, fraudulent activities will not lessen. It is noted that detection comprises three parts, namely, financial statement audit, focused risk assessment, and examination of management overrides. However, accounting fraud remains a significant concern for the audit profession. Hence, it is vital to create an audit plan that will enable the auditor to discover any deficiencies in the system that may permit fraud. The established methods for helping audit planning are the maintenance of a fraud policy, a fraud vulnerability review, an anonymous hotline, and extensive background checks.

Employees should attest to having understood the fraud policy, which should be underpinned with training workshops and periodic reviews as it may dampen accounting fraud. Fraud vulnerability reviews analyze the extent of fraud risk to the company, including the location of assets and how they could be stolen. In addition, there should be an anonymous hotline where internal and external stakeholders can report fraudulent activities in a safe space. Unfortunately, personnel files are not adequately maintained, so there should be secondary checks to ensure that initial information supplied at the application, such as education or work experience, is correct as a measure to weed out potential fraudsters.

It is the function of management to create a system of prevention and detection, which is best achieved when compliance systems are at the heart of the business. **It is asserted that** if the following conditions are implemented, namely, transparency of policies and procedures, effective communication, and performance-related pay for all employees, then the risk of fraud should fall drastically. However, *management override* is viewed as the *Achilles's heel* of fraud prevention and results in damaging collusive fraud such as Enron. Therefore, fraud prevention must be instituted at all levels in the organization, including senior management. The detection of management override usually results from anonymous tips underscoring the importance of an anonymous hotline.

The Importance of Internal Controls

Accounting information, or, more precisely, financial statements, allows the allocation of scarce resources in an economy underpinned by internal controls, which is associated with the opportunity side of the fraud triangle. Hence, an opportunity is discovered appropriate internal controls can help detect a fraud.

It is maintained that an internal control is part of a system of internal controls for an organization that is established by senior management, including internal checking, auditing, and other controls that allow the reliable functioning of a business. **Nijenhuis (2016)** describes five key features that are present in most internal control systems, namely, control environment, risk assessment, control activities, information and communication, and monitoring, which collectively lead to a strong internal control system. The correct application of an internal control system ensures the safeguarding of assets and the veracity of records and leads to an efficient and effective control environment. **It is suggested that** an effective internal control system is one of the major steps taken by an entity toward the prevention of fraud and by extension accounting fraud.

It has been established that a robust internal control system enhances corporate governance, raises management performance, and dampens fraud because the entire workforce is involved in the detection of fraud. In contrast, weak internal controls not only lead to fraud but also raise the control risk, which is the risk of internal controls not preventing or detecting misstatements that provide assurance for an organization's assets and records.

Ethical Culture

An ethical culture can be defined as "the perception about the conditions that are in place in the organization to comply or not comply with what constitutes unethical and ethical behavior." An ethical culture in conjunction with sound internal controls ensures a greater degree of prevention. Internal control provides the tools to detect fraud, whereas an ethical culture creates an environment where it is perceived by everyone that fraud is wrong. An ethical culture undermines the rationalization of fraud, as per the fraud triangle, as it signals to employees that fraud is erroneous. Ethical business environments provide deterrence because hiding fraudulent acts will become increasingly challenging and punishment is guaranteed once the fraudster is apprehended.

A study by **KPMG Forensic (2014)** stated that a CEO should lead by example and create a highly ethical and honest culture that will pay dividends in the long run. A study found a strong correlation between companies that had an ethical culture and stronger performance in comparison with their competitors. **Arjoon (2005, 349)** states that "ethics is truly an essential ingredient for business success," as demonstrated by another study that suggested that employee commitment increases in an ethical environment.

Red Flags of Accounting Fraud

As discussed earlier, all three conditions of the fraud triangle, namely pressure, opportunity, and rationalization, must exist before a fraud will potentially take place. Consequently, the key to preventing fraud is *breaking* the fraud triangle.

A red flag is one or more conditions that are abnormal in nature or differ from the norm. It is an indication that something is wrong and should be further investigated. The author will begin with generalities, or what is referred to as *soft red flags,* and move on to specific accounting, or what the author regards as *hard red flags.*

Common internal control weaknesses that can operate as red flags include:

- Deficient segregation of duties
- Inadequate physical safeguards
- Unsatisfactory independent checks
- Improper authorization of documents and records
- Override of existing controls
- A faulty accounting system

Analytical irregularities are relationships that do not make sense and that appear to be unreasonable. These include large or small transactions that occur at strange times that may involve personnel not normally associated with them. Examples of analytical irregularities include:

- Company assets sold below market value
- Many bank accounts
- Downsizing in a healthy economy
- Unexpected overdrafts or shortages of cash

Operational anomalies are curious events concerning a company's operations. Although they may not be within the control of management, they warrant attention as a red flag for possible fraud. Some of these anomalies are

- shortage of capital;
- repeated changes in lawyers or seeking multiple expert opinions;
- frequent changes in senior management;
- high staff turnover;
- and significant changes in employee attitude or lifestyle.

As cash is the most stolen asset, accountants should focus attention on the red flags of cash embezzlement and accounts receivable, and these may include an unnecessary number of voids:

- Discounts, and returns
- Unexpected activity in an inactive bank account
- Customer complaints about notices for defaulting or nonpayment of accounts
- Inconsistencies between bank deposits and deposits posted to the company records
- An unusual quantity or extent of expense items or reimbursements to staff or senior management
- Unusual cash transactions
- Frequent write-offs of accounts receivable
- An increase in the allowance of doubtful accounts

Payroll is normally an automated or outsourced function that is open to collusion and fraud. Red flags in this area include the following:

- Overtime claimed during a quiet period or by staff who would not normally do so

- Negative and material variations between standard and actual wages
- Staff with little or no payroll deductions
- *Ghost employees*

Purchasing or procurement results in a significant outflow of monies within most companies and is susceptible to fraud. Similarly, an organization's inventory can be vulnerable to theft. Red flags indicating that the procurement and inventory functions are being manipulated include:

- A rising number of complaints regarding products or services
- An increase in the purchasing of inventory but no growth in sales
- Peculiar inventory reduction
- The proliferation of scrap items and reorders for the same materials
- And surplus or slow-moving inventory

As noted in earlier sections, the rationale for manipulating the financial reporting function or engaging in accounting fraud is different from the embezzlement of company assets. Accounting fraud does not result in an explicit financial advantage to one individual. Instead, it supplies an implicit gain in the shape of higher share prices, superior stock options for managers, and continued lines of credit. However, red flags are often present in accounting fraud, just as they are in asset misuse schemes. The following are some of the red flags seen in accounting fraud:

- Aggressive revenue recognition
- Extraordinary and profitable transactions toward the end of reporting periods
- Boosting profits by selling undervalued assets or recording one-time events as operating income
- Persistent negative cash flows while reporting positive or growing profits

- Expenses rising quicker than revenues or sales
- Use of misleading classifications
- Capitalizing operating costs
- Pressure to report positive or growing profits
- Material and growing transactions with related parties
- Regularly changing accounting policies such as depreciation technique
- Using special purpose entities (SPEs) to improve gearing

As an early warning system (EWS), the aforementioned flags indicate the potential for accounting fraud. A dated yet robust study confirms that red flags are a cost-effective EWS that may be used to detect and thwart accounting fraud.

Governmental Regulation

To protect the global capital markets from recurring fraud, rules and regulations are required. Moreover, for capital markets to operate efficiently, the quality, reliability, and integrity of financial statements supplied by companies to the market must be true and fair. Therefore, we will briefly explore the Sarbanes–Oxley Act 2002 (SOX-2002), which was instituted in the United States as a response to the menace of accounting fraud.

At the turn of the 21st century, the United States experienced major accounting scandals such as Enron, WorldCom, and Tyco that resulted in severe socioeconomic damage. The table, Figure 2.6, highlights the asset size of the Top 10 bankruptcies to date (**Frunza 2016, 394**):

This led to growing calls for reform of business practices and accounting standards for listed companies that culminated in SOX-2002. SOX-2002 reporting lists a body of rules and regulations that are designed to align the interests of management and shareholders and reduce the risk of fraudulent activity.

SOX-2002 was supposed to enhance the corporate governance of listed companies and, crucially, the confidence of investors in U.S. capital markets. Researchers found that SOX-2002 had improved the quality of financial information supplied to the public and that to a

Rank	Company	Date	Country	Sector	Assets ($B)
1	Lehman	15.09.08	United States	Investment Bank	691
2	Washington Mutual, Inc.	26.08.08	United States	Savings & Loan Holding Co	328
3	WorldCom, Inc.	21.07.02	United States	Telecommunications	104
4	General Motors	6.01.09	United States	Manufactures & Sells Motor Vehicles	91
5	Kaupthing Bank	9.10.08	Iceland	Banking	87
6	CIT Group, Inc.	11.01.09	United States	Banking Holding Co.	80
7	Enron Corp.	12.01.01	United States	Energy Trading, Natural Gas	66
8	Conseco, Inc.	17.12.02	United States	Financial Services Holding Co.	61
9	Chrysler, LLC	30.04.09	United States	Manufactures & Sells Motor Vehicles	39
10	Thornburg Mortgage, Inc.	5.01.09	United States	Residential mortgage	37

Figure 2.6 Top ten bankruptcies to date

large degree investor confidence in financial reporting and the capital markets had been restored. **Hochberg et al.** (**2009, 575**) stated that SOX-2002 had "improved disclosure, transparency, and corporate governance, thereby reducing misconduct and mismanagement by insiders, and that for shareholders overall, *these benefits may outweigh the costs of compliance.*" The final point regarding costs of compliance is important as foreign companies may be deterred from entering American capital markets in view of the excessive burden of compliance. Also, it has been observed that post SOX-2002, companies are more careful with their spending.

However, as already noted, despite changes to regulation, monitoring by various market stakeholders, such as academics and commentators, and improvements in the prevention and detection of accounting fraud, the phenomenon continues, and the authors believe it has only worsened. Consequently, the authors decided to explore the dark triad, which may explain if a certain type of person may potentially undertake accounting fraud.

Dark Triad

Epstein and Ramamoorti (**2016**) argue that in the face of the dark triad personality types, the Cressey fraud triangle collapses into a *single* *dimension*, namely, opportunity. So, what is the dark triad? Recent research has highlighted three nonstandard (or deviant) personality types or categories whose behaviors may help explain accounting fraud. These personality types have been designated narcissism, Machiavellianism, and psychopathy, that is, the dark triad, see Figure 2.7.

Narcissistic people are grandiose, prideful egotists who demonstrate deficient empathy toward others. These individuals are obsessed with power and prestige and are incapable of seeing the damage this causes to themselves and others. The **Machiavellian** personality is strategic, deeply cynical, inclined toward deception, and utilizes other people to achieve their ambitions. Lastly, the **psychopath** is short of empathy and will not hesitate to engage in dangerous and reckless behavior. All three personality types share themes of "deceitfulness, self-promotion, coldness, disagreeableness, exploitation and aggression" (Furnham et al. 2013). Psychopathy is considered the most sinister personality trait of the dark triad and will be explored in greater depth by the authors in the next chapter.

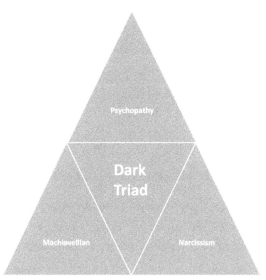

Figure 2.7 The dark Triad

Source: Adapted by authors.

Dark Triad CEOs and CFOs

The business world is littered with dark triad fraudsters such as *Chainsaw Al Dunlap*, CEO of Scott Paper, and, finally, Sunbeam Products, who showed no remorse when making thousands of redundancies and were branded a psychopath. *Crazy* Eddie Antar was a self-confessed psychopath; however, he used this portrayal to gain a reduced sentence for his fraud. Aaron Beam, a CFO who engineered the HealthSouth's fraud, accused the CEO, Richard Scrushy, of being a psychopath. The notorious Enron CFO, Andrew Fastow, has been characterized as being a narcissist.

Research indicates that senior management contains a greater degree of dark triad personalities in comparison with society at large. It has been hypothesized that the frequency of psychopaths on Wall Street may be more than 10 percent. Given the high degree of pervasiveness of psychopaths in the business world, **Epstein and Ramamoorti (2016)** argued that external auditors should incorporate the "Dark Triad personality risk" feature into their formal risk evaluations and protocols. Because auditors remain ill-informed about the potential incidence of such personality types, there is a greater likelihood of accounting fraud that will be elaborated further chapter exploring blockchain technology.

The dark triad helps to explain why some fraudsters are motivated to commit accounting fraud, in contrast to *accidental or situational fraudsters*, who yield to pressure when the occasion arises and even these *accidental or situational fraudsters* will eventually normalize their behavior. According to the sociology literature, this is known as the *normalization of deviance*.

Relevance of Dark Triad to Fraud Prevention and Detection

As discussed earlier, the theory of fraud detection and prevention is normally structured in the shape of the fraud triangle and its variations. The fraud triangle model suggests that three conditions must be present for a fraudulent activity: a motive for the deed, a supposed opportunity to execute the deed, and a standpoint that allows the fraudster to rationalize the deed.

Psychopaths may also impact the other remaining sides of the fraud triangle, namely, pressure and opportunity. Internal control mechanisms based on the threat of detection and retribution lower apparent opportunity. On the other hand, psychopaths are usually fearless and self-assured in their capability to maneuver their way out of punishment. The MICE model further reveals the pressure side of the triangle. Psychopaths are normally selfish and have a grandiose sense of entitlement that may motivate fraud. **Babiak and O'Toole (2012)** noted that psychopaths are prone to *thrill-seeking* behavior, which may itself be an inducement to commit fraud. According to Bailey (2015), psychopaths "know right from wrong, but do not care."

Thus, far we explored the preeminent fraud model, the fraud triangle, and its variations, which help to explain why fraud and accounting fraud occur. We argue that although there have been advances in the **prevention, deterrence, and detection** including improvements in global auditing standards and government regulation, accounting fraud persists. Hence, chapter three will explore the psychopathic side of the dark triad in greater depth and discuss whether it can be modeled to predict psychopathic tendencies in corporate psychopath accountants.

CHAPTER 3

Accounting Fraud and Corporate Psychopathy

Modeling the Corporate Psychopath Accountant

> *I take full responsibility for what happened at Enron. But saying that, I know in my mind that I did nothing criminal.*
>
> —Kenneth Lay, Former CEO of Enron

Dark triad theory will shortly be explored in greater detail which comprises Machiavellianism, narcissism, and psychopathy. Since, the authors believe a better understanding of these negative traits, especially in the work environment, will empower organizations to identify and hopefully contain these people. Narcissistic individuals are preoccupied with their own manifestation and personal success, regardless of how that impacts the organization. Machiavellians are highly focused people who obsessively pursue outcomes regardless of the means used to reach them, irrespective of whether they are legal or ethical.

A psychopath is someone who exhibits a lack of conscience, is egotistical, and whose approach to life is merciless and characterized by personal advance at the detriment of others. It is believed that approximately 1 percent of individuals display psychopathic personality behaviors; although it may be as high as 3.5 to 4 percent for senior-level corporate workers and, more explicitly, CEOs. Corporate psychopaths are people showing psychopathic tendencies who function in the corporate sector (**Boddy 2010**). It is maintained that the corporate world is a magnet for psychopaths due to their drive for success and power, characteristics that often lead to high financial rewards and senior-level management positions. It is argued that the motive of shareholder maximization at the sacrifice of other objectives encourages psychopathic people to ascend the mountain of success. In fact, psychopaths can and do effortlessly survive and, very often, perform successfully in a corporate environment, staying under the radar of corporate detection. Corporate psychopaths potentially account for an excessively large proportion of damaging and immoral business practices. Studies have demonstrated correlations in the general population highlighting individuals with psychopathic personalities who are guilty of criminal and violent behavior. It is argued that corporate psychopaths possess the capacity to *wreak havoc* on businesses and negatively impact business performance including on employees.

Dark Triad Theory

The dark triad is a psychological theory of personality that was established by **Paulhus and Williams (2002)** that describes three especially unpleasant, but nonpathological personality types: Machiavellianism, "sub-clinical narcissistic personality disorder" (narcissism), and "sub-clinical anti-social personality disorder" (psychopathy). Individually, these personality types are referred to as *dark* because each kind is believed to contain malevolent or evil qualities.

All three dark triad characteristics are conceptually discrete although there is empirical evidence that highlights that they intersect. These nefarious traits are correlated with an insensitive and deeply unscrupulous interpersonal style.

- Narcissism is distinguished by vanity, arrogance, egotism, and deficient empathy.
- Machiavellianism is demonstrated by negative influence and exploitation of others, a lack of morality, insensitivity, and supreme self-interest.

- Psychopathy is displayed by selfishness, lack of remorse, impulsiveness, and lack of any kind of care.

High scores in these negative traits, which are discussed in greater depth later, have been found to statistically increase a person's probability to undertake crimes, produce social suffering, and create acute problems for organizations, especially if they are in positions of authority. Overall, these individuals are likely to be less compassionate, reasonable, empathetic, content, and have any humanity. The authors will further explore psychopathy as it may be linked to accounting fraud.

It is maintained that psychopathy is a personality condition, underpinned by traits including artificial charm, deceit, prone to impulsivity, deficient remorse, and absence of empathy, which may cause a psychopathic individual to be incarcerated for committing criminal acts. Psychopaths tend to be the most studied groups, specifically by psychologists and psychiatrists. Many people wrongly believe psychopathy to be a mental illness, when actually it is a personality disorder; basically, these individual's brains are literally wired differently. Functional magnetic resonance imaging research has confirmed that psychopaths do not have the capability to experience fundamental human emotions such as feelings of guilt, compunction, or empathy; instead, the psychopath will feign sincerity and manipulate others for their own advantage. As already noted, 1 percent of the general will display psychopathic tendencies and related aberrant behaviors; and senior management will contain 3.5 to 4 percent. Individuals showing the traits of psychopathy are less likely to be trusted, overly ambitious, even backstabbers but are not considered as dangerous corporate psychopaths possessing the capacity to adversely impact organizational performance. It has been noted that psychopaths are "attracted to fast-paced, transitional organizations that can offer high potential for rewards, a stimulating environment and cover for their dubious actions" (**Andrews and Furniss 2009**). Another dark trait of psychopaths is "their ability to portray themselves as benevolent and charming," making it challenging to recognize who really is a psychopath or who is not (**Bakan 2008, 26**). It has been acknowledged that psychopaths can function successfully in organizations without detection because they seem to be normal and even appear to have suitable qualities. Consequently, they are more than likely to be found in senior leadership and management positions, wielding enormous power and ability to affect many employees.

The term Machiavellianism was created because it was supposedly encouraged by the medieval Niccolo Machiavelli in his treatise, *The Prince*. A Machiavellian individual is characterized as being ruthless, selfish, cold, and manipulative and shares many traits with a psychopath because he or she "has no reference to moral standards, promotes the idea that the end justifies the means ... and advocates the use of force if deemed necessary to achieve desired ends" (**Boddy 2010, 301**). As already noted, Machiavellianism is a personality disorder where the individual is cynical and gives high regard to competition, money, and power; it is worryingly associated with a higher frequency of bullying in the workplace and, in general, engaging in unethical behavior.

Narcissism was initially developed by the leading psychiatrist Freud, and the concept of narcissism was originated from

the myth of Narcissus, a beautiful young man who, spurning the affection of various nymphs, was fated by a goddess to fall into unrequited love. Narcissus spent his life looking at his reflection in the water, eventually starving to death by his own misfortune (**Boddy 2010, 302**).

Consequently, the modern connotation of this myth is "as being someone who loves themselves too much for their own good" (**Boddy 2010, 302**).

The Corporate Psychopath

The modern corporation is defined as a self-serving entity, which behaves analogously like a *person*, as it can hold noncurrent assets including property and undertake contracts. It is argued that the primary objective of a corporation namely shareholder wealth maximization can lead to undesirable consequences such as poor labor conditions and corporate law and regulations facilitate a public corporation behaving like a corporate psychopath. Consequently, the authors argue that the corporation may breed corporate psychopaths who "are motivated by a desire to win, a desire for power and a desire to gain wealth and prestige" (**Boddy 2010, 308**). The term *corporate psychopath* is used to define the individuals with psychopathic traits operating in the corporate sector. Corporate psychopaths have also been termed *successful psychopaths* because they have managed to avoid legal authorities and the mental health system because they do not commit violent and criminal acts, unlike their criminal psychopath cousins. The corporate sector will always attract corporate psychopaths due to the power and wealth, especially at the senior management level this sector generates. It is argued that as they climb the corporate ladder their psychopathic tendencies will be amplified. Eventually, they will achieve these senior positions as their personal interests are usually divergent to the long-term interests of internal and external stakeholders.

The Successful Corporate Psychopath

The preceding section suggests that the corporate psychopath is *successful* since, they may display the characteristics of psychopathy, however, are successful in their actions but crucially avoid being discovered. It is argued that successful psychopaths are able to change at will to social environments, which is deficient in *unsuccessful psychopaths*. In fact, it is suggested that certain psychopathic characteristics can be positive within certain settings, for example, climbing the corporate ladder. It has been extensively noted in the literature that the strong appearance of successful psychopaths is prevalent in the legal, political, and business arenas due to the lack of detection and punishment mechanisms.

It has been established that *successful* psychopaths tend to score lower on social deviance scales and much higher on executive functioning tests. This implies that *successful* psychopaths can function in a socially acceptable manner, which serves as a method of self-protection. In contrast, *unsuccessful* psychopaths overwhelmingly show their psychopath characteristics due to lack of control. Successful psychopaths were also discovered to score considerably higher in heart rate response to social stressors—suggesting some level of societal and social perception. It is suggested that superior executive functioning gives a measure of protection to successful psychopaths which prevents them from being caught.

The Psychopathic Process

It is acknowledged that there is a distinct psychopathic process that charts a corporate psychopath's career trajectory. Initially, psychopaths will *infiltrate* an organization behaving like a model employee, climbing the corporate ladder by actively manipulating powerful individuals by building relationships with them and crucially exploiting these relationships for their benefit.

Psychopaths are adept at pigeonholing their lives, thus making it difficult to identify and root them out of corporations, especially at the hiring stage. Paradoxically, organizations attempt to recruit individuals who display certain attractive characteristics, many of which are visible in psychopaths who craft the ideal image of a perfect employee; they make an extremely positive first impression and routinely manipulate the recruiters in the interview process with their superficial charm and hyper energy.

Many psychopaths use blatant deception and lie to manufacture outstanding résumés and stellar work experiences, also constructing performance awards and fake references to help them succeed in obtaining their employment. In fact, "psychopathic traits can be observed to a greater or lesser degree when promotion opportunities arise—individuals ... may suddenly display what might be described as psychopathic behaviour, in order to draw positive attention to themselves" (**Andrews and Furniss 2009, 24**). Psychopaths are usually charming toward individuals in positions of authority so that they may be exploited later and, in contrast, are callous with their peers and subordinates.

Finally, "psychopaths will discard individuals once their utility is spent and these people may also come to oppose the psychopath," damaging the work environment (**Andrews and Furniss 2009, 23**). Eventually, when psychopaths achieve high office, they create an organization where power is concentrated with a few people and everyone else in the organization finds themselves abandoned or may be unemployed.

There is strong evidence that suggests corporate psychopaths are deeply destructive to their organizations and the people they work with. Psychopaths are opportunistic and disruptive, if not unsettling, individuals who damage workplace productivity and efficiency.

Empirical research clearly indicates that psychopaths create a toxic workplace underpinned by conflict, bullying of others, poor job satisfaction, and frequent organizational constraints. Research has established that the psychopaths can potentially damage organizational development especially new hires or junior staff as they are deemed to be disruptive. This is an important point since, according to social learning theory, people identify and copy the behaviors of others, especially in senior leadership positions, and may view these psychopaths as successful and worthy of emulation.

Corporate Psychopath Accountants

Psychopaths are usually fearless and self-assured in their capability to maneuver their way out of punishment. The money, ideology, coercion, and ego or entitlement model further reveal the pressure side of the fraud triangle. Psychopaths are normally selfish and have a grandiose sense of entitlement that may motivate fraud. It has been noted that psychopaths are prone to *thrill-seeking* behavior, which may itself be an inducement for fraud. According to **Bailey (2015)**, psychopaths "know right from wrong, but do not care."

Robert Hare worked with Canadian convicts and developed the respected standard clinical test of psychopathy, the Psychopathy Checklist, Revised. Psychopathy is a personality disorder that has at least two features or factors:

- Factor 1, or "primary," psychopathy includes an inclination to lie, lack of remorse, callousness, and manipulativeness. These tendencies are usually facilitated by superficial charm.
- Factor 2, or "secondary," psychopathy includes impulsivity, intolerance of frustration, quick-temperedness, and lack of long-term goals.

Factor 1 is of concern to the present study as it covers the characteristics that are predictive of fraud. Factor 2 is more than likely to result in imprisonment although it is seen to flare up in cases of business executives. Primary psychopathy is "generally viewed as the core of the psychopathy construct" (**Lee and Ashton 2005, 1576**).

Bailey (2017) argues that of the dark triad, the psychopathic tendency has a direct effect on the rationalization of the fraud triangle. Psychopaths may also impact the other remaining sides of the fraud triangle, namely, pressure and opportunity. Internal control mechanisms based on the threat of detection and retribution lower apparent opportunity. Therefore, the authors will attempt to establish a *CORPORATE PSYCHOPATH EQUATION* that will potentially model psychopath tendencies in corporate accountants and auditors.

Bailey (2017) has already conducted a study with American accounting students that used the Levenson's Self-Report Psychopathy Scale (LSRP). This scale comprises 26 statements, with participants required to rate their agreement with the statement on a Likert scale from (1) strongly disagree to (5) strongly agree. This investigation concluded that accounting students scored relatively low on the psychopathy scale. In another investigation, again utilizing Levenson's instrument, **Bailey (2015)** reported a significant effect of psychopathy on academic accountants' research publication count, mediated by an enlarged approval of unethical practices. This study concurred with a situation-based study that established an increased readiness to accept unethical behaviors, reconciled by moral disconnection; therefore, **Bailey's (2015)** study suggests a link between psychopathy and a real behavioral result.

The authors believe that **Bailey (2017)** *has not effectively explored the link between Accounting Fraud and psychopathy* and *neither offered a solution and states* "It is important to recognize that psychopathic tendencies exist among students and professionals, given the potential for harm, more research is warranted." Hence, the authors will test the potential psychopath predisposition among professional accountants in a Top 10 global accounting firm.

The authors intend to undertake a quantitative study using a variation of the LSRP psychology survey including questions around organizational culture that may be a breeding ground for corporate psychopaths. There is no evidence to suggest that the participants will be in any personal or professional danger. **Bailey (2015, 2017)** states "… that research participants are willing to give frank responses to sensitive or incriminating questions when they are confident of anonymity."

The authors believe this study to be important since, research into corporate psychopathy has indicated the rise of a darker facet of leadership within the workplace that comprises deception, harassment, and aggression. Employee job satisfaction is damaged along with heightened psychological suffering. This point is very important since the average person spends one-third of their life or 90,000 c hours in the workplace, consequently, the effect of malfunctional or a toxic workplace will undoubtedly have an adverse and may be a lasting impact on a worker's life. Moreover, abusive leadership has been associated with inferior work performance productivity and the bottom line, that is, profitability. It is argued that this all has a cost and psychopathic behavior has been linked to workplace deviance, costing organizations billions in financial losses.

Modeling the Corporate Psychopath Accountant

The authors conducted a study using a questionnaire on a sample of qualified accountants, from a global Top 10 firm with offices based in the Asia and Asia Pacific region. It should be noted that this is the first time in the literature that professionals are taking a questionnaire that is explicitly attempting to model corporate accountant psychopathy.

The questionnaire comprised four sections covering baseline questions, culture, unethical accounting practices/accounting fraud that was the *disapproval variable*, psychopathy scores, and finally deterrence of accounting fraud. The second section was unique as the authors wanted to ascertain whether culture was a factor in creating corporate psychopathy.

The authors were helped by an internal director of audit who circulated the questionnaire through Survey Monkey, which included participant consent in April 2022. The cut-off for completed questionnaires was late May 2022, and the authors received 61 anonymously completed questionnaires; however, four had to be ignored as they were incomplete, thus the total sample was 57.

The key highlights from the baseline analysis or Section A are:

- In all, 89 percent of the sample was aged between 24 and 55 years and above.
- Overall, 54 percent were male respondents and the balance, 46 percent, were female.
- All the respondents were professionally qualified including 22 who were multicertified, that is, they held more than one professional qualification such as Association of Chartered Certified Accountants (ACCA) and Institute of Chartered Accountants of Pakistan (ICAP).
- The participants ranged from audit junior to partner.
- In all, 47 participants specialized in audit, one in corporate finance, six in tax, and three in business advisory services.
- Overall, 53 percent of the sample had 5- to 10-year professional experience, and 30 percent of participants had more than 10 years of professional experience.
- In all, 75 percent explicitly stated that they adhered to a recognized ethical framework such as Islam or Buddhism or Christianity and the balance answered *other*.

Section B explored the corporate culture of the firm as the authors wanted to establish whether this is an explanatory variable for modeling the corporate psychopath accountant.

Corporate culture signifies the beliefs and behaviors that govern how an organization's employees and management interact and conduct external transactions. Most of the time, corporate culture is implicit, may develop incrementally over time, and is underpinned by the critical characteristics of the worker the company hires.

The term *corporate culture* highlights the beliefs and practices related with a particular organization. For example, corporate culture may be highlighted in the way a firm hire and promotes employees, or in its corporate vision statement. Some companies attempt to align themselves with a specific set of values or ethics, such as by expressing themselves as an *innovative* or *environmentally conscious* business. For example, Alphabet Inc. or Google is famous for promoting an employee-centric culture where its workers are permitted to spend up to 20 percent of a company pursuing their own projects. In contrast, Amazon is known for its unrelenting quest for superior customer service and exceptional operational productivity.

It is argued that corporate cultures, whether they are molded proactively or achieved organically, are at the crux of a company's ideology and practice, and affect every facet of a business, from each employee welfare or retention to brand image. Consequently, as noted earlier, a corporate psychopath can influence the business culture.

The seminal study by **Harvard *Business Review* (2015)** highlighted six vital features of a healthy corporate culture. Beginning with a *vision*: from an uncomplicated mission statement, a company's vision is considered to be a powerful instrument. For example, Pepsi's notorious business slogan: "Beat Coca Cola" is a brilliant corporate vision. Second, *values*, although an all-encompassing concept, represent the mindset and perceptions essential to achieve a company vision.

Equally, *practices* are the visible methods, underpinned by ethics, through which a company realizes its values. For example, Netflix stresses the significance of knowledge-focused, high-performing employees; therefore, Netflix remunerates its employees with the highest possible salaries, rather than through a pay grade where an employee will have to climb the corporate ladder. Next are "People", with companies employing and recruiting employees who are strongly aligned to their corporate culture. As noted earlier in the psychopathic process section, a future psychopath is a master of feigning sincerity and deceiving colleagues.

Finally, *narrative* and *place* that are distinctly modern perhaps the most contemporary features of a corporate culture. Possessing a powerful narrative or *origin story*, such as that of Bill Gates of Microsoft, is imperative for development and a positive public image. The *place* of business, such as office space or staff facilities, is probably one of the major innovations in contemporary corporate culture. Although outside the scope of this study the current global phenomenon of agile working, postpandemic has changed the concept of *place*.

Figure 3.1 represents 12 statements that were tested on a Likert scale, 1 to 5, ranging from completely agree (moderately agree, unclear) to (moderately disagree) completely disagree.

Question	Statement	Positive Outcome	Neutral
1	Teamwork is encouraged and rewarded.	X	
2	People's behaviour is not governed by office policies, procedures, and manuals.		X
3	Completing an assignment to budget even if that involves unpaid overtime is discouraged.		X
4	Work-life balance is actively promoted in the office.		X
5	Staff are not encouraged to take leave / vacation / holiday.	X	
6	You feel valued and supported by your line manager in your job function.	X	
7	You believe that senior management do not work for the benefit of your office rather for themselves.	X	
8	Promotion is open, fair and transparent.	X	
9	Authority is more important than job satisfaction.		X
10	Workplace stress should be managed so that it does not damage health.	X	
11	You are likely to recommend your firm to others.	X	
12	Diversity and inclusion are the priority agenda at your firm.	X	

Figure 3.1 Culture statements

Once the Cronbach's alpha, a measure of internal consistency, for this part of the survey, was established at an acceptable 0.63. The authors subjected all 12 questions to a null (where the population mean is equal to 3) and research hypothesis (where the population mean does not equal 3) underpinned by the confidence interval and one-test statistical tests.

In summary, the participants significantly agreed in a positive manner toward Questions 1, 5, 6 to 8, and 10 to 12 and neither agreed or disagreed to Questions 2 to 4 and 9, see Figure 3.1. Suggesting that the firm should consider improving office protocols, workload, work–life balance, and job satisfaction ideally in consultation with firm employees. On the other hand, there is much to commend as the corporate culture is based on teamwork, staff well-being, employees feel valued, there is a belief that senior managers work for the benefit of the firm, progression is fair and transparent, workplace stress is not tolerated, the firm would be recommended by its workers, and is considered to be an inclusive and diverse work environment.

Overall, it is a good corporate culture as the mean culture score was 32 compared ideal or perfect score of 28 (where participants responded completely agree or completely disagree based upon the statement). Whether the corporate culture is a factor in creating a corporate psychopath accountant will be demonstrated later in the multiple regression or modeling section.

Section C explored disapproval toward unethical actions, the first four statements comprised basic accounting fraud, and the remaining four were behavioral in nature. Like Section A, a Likert scale, 1 to 5, ranging from completely agree (moderately agree, unclear) to (moderately disagree) complete disagree was used in Figure 3.2.

Once the Cronbach's alpha, a measure of internal consistency, for Section B, was established at an acceptable 0.89. The author subjected all eight questions to a null (where the population mean is equal to 3) and research hypothesis (where the population mean does not equal 3) underpinned by the confidence interval and one-t test statistical tests. In brief, the participants significantly disagreed with all eight statements suggesting that even if they were suffering from lifestyle pressure, as per the pressure side of the fraud triangle, they would not undertake accounting fraud, such as inflating revenue or selling a company client list.

Question	Statement	Disagreed
1	To improve revenue, management decided to record fictitious credit sales. (Impact: Higher revenue, receivables & profit)	X
2	Hiding most of the scrap expense in other expense accounts to avoid scrutiny of excessive scrap costs. (Impact: Individual expense not faithfully representing the business)	X
3	Request a legal firm to delay invoicing a material amount of work already undertaken until the next financial year end and it is not accrued for. (Impact: Defer expenses to improve profitability)	X
4	Postpone writing off spoiled, worthless inventory. (Impact: Overstating closing inventory leading to higher profits)	X
5	The employee chooses not to report an over payment of $500 included in their monthly pay, due to a clerical error.	X
6	The employee deposits a cheque, received in payment of a written-off receivable account from more than two years ago, into their own personal bank account.	X
7	The employee goes to see a client and overclaims mileage.	X
8	The employee sells the company's client list to a competitor.	X

Figure 3.2 Unethical actions

Question	Statement
1	Success is based on the survival of the fittest; I am not concerned about the losers.
2	For me, what's right is whatever I can get away with.
3	In today's world, I feel justified in doing anything I can get away with, to succeed.
4	My main purpose in life is getting as many goodies as I can.
5	Making a lot of money is my most important goal.
6	I let others worry about higher values; my main concern is with the profit
7	People who are stupid enough to get ripped off usually deserve it
8	Looking out for myself is my top priority
9	I tell other people what they want to hear so that they will do what I want them to do.
10	I would be upset if my success came at someone else's expense.
11	I often admire a clever scam.
12	I make a point of trying not to hurt others, in pursuit of my goals.
13	I enjoy manipulating other people's feelings.
14	I feel bad if my words or actions cause someone else to feel emotional pain.
15	Even if I were trying very hard to sell something, I would not tell untruths about it.
16	Cheating is not justified because it is unfair to others.

Figure 3.3 Statements testing psychopathy

Section D measured the psychopathy of the participants using 16 questions. Again a Likert scale, 1 to 5, was used ranging from disagree strongly to agree strongly, Figure 3.3.

According to the primary study (Brinkley et al. 2000), the following thresholds were recognized:

- **0–48: nonpsychopathic group**
- **49–57: mixed group;**
- **≥ 58: psychopathic group.**

The results of the sample of 57 professional accountants are shown in Figure 3.4.

It is interesting to note that a *nonpsychopathic group* **of 36** included **four accountants who had a score of 48 and could be argued to be borderline** *mixed group* cases. There were **17 clear cases in the** *mixed group*, and although this is a small study, the mean, 45.84, and standard deviation, 7.72, were much higher than Bailey's (2017) study (mean = 28.05, standard deviation = 6.03), although the sample size was more than 200 albeit they were students. The Cronbach alpha for Section C was established at an acceptable 0.71.

Hare (1994) reported that approximately 1 percent of the general population meet the clinical threshold for psychopath and later maintained (Babiak and Hare 2019) that the incidence of psychopaths was higher in the business world. This study of 57 highlighted that 7 percent, or 4 participants, were corporate psychopath accountants and

Psychopathy Score	Participants	Percentage
0-48	37	64
49-57	17	29
≥58	4	7
Total	57	100

Figure 3.4 Results

30 percent, or 17 contributors, have borderline or mixed psychopathy which could become problematic in the future.

In Section E, 91 percent of the accountants believe that a large fine and lengthy prison is a potential deterrence for accounting fraud.

Based on the results, the authors created a multiple regression (Rxy) model that could predict psychopathy, Y criterion, by using several predictors in combination:

X1—Mean Disapproval of Unethical Actions
X2—Culture
X3—Gender
X4—Professional Experience of more than 10 years

Each predictor is *weighted* in a different manner according to its discrete correlation with Y and its correlation with the other predictors. The objective of multiple correlation is to supply a regression equation that will weight each predictor variable in such a way that the combination of the X variables does a much better role in predicting Y or psychopathy than any single X variable in isolation.

The reason for selecting X1 and X2 has been discussed earlier and X3 and X4 were chosen as it is being hypothesized that gender and professional experience of more than 10 years may be an explanatory variable in predicting corporate psychopathy. Although 75 percent of the participants followed a religious framework such as Christianity or Islam, it was decided not to use this as an explanatory variable as it was not clear if the *Other* category of balance followed an alternative practice or did not follow an ethical framework.

Predictor	Score
X1 – Mean Disapproval of Unethical Actions	3
X2 – Culture	33
X3 – Gender (M=1, F=0)	M / 1
X4 – Professional Experience > 10 years (Y=1, N=0)	N / 0

Figure 3.5 Hypothetical accountant profile

According to the summary output, the multiple regression model predicting criterion Y or psychopathy is (as per practice the figures are to four significant figures):

$$Y = a + b1X1 + b2X2 + b3X3 + b4X4$$

$$Y = 59.1060 - 2.5840X1 + 0.0336X2 - 0.4386X3 - 7.9113X4$$

Consequently, if we have the hypothetical accountant profile as shown in Figure 3.5, then the predicted score for psychopathy would be,

$$Y = 59.1060 - 2.5840*3 + 0.0336*33 - 0.4386*1 - 7.9113*0$$
$$\text{Result} = 52$$
(To the nearest whole number)

Interestingly, if the hypothetical accountant profile had experience of more than 10 years then the result would be 44 and this person would be in the nonpsychopathic group, suggesting that experienced accountants with more than 10 years' experience may have less psychopathic tendencies.

The final step in the multiple regression model is to ascertain the correlation between all of the salient variables that occur in the multiple regression equation. This was achieved in the study by finding the correlation between each of the four pairs of variables, and the *correlation matrix* was calculated using the Excel pack, which also appears at the bottom of the summary output. This matrix encapsulates, see Figure 3.6,

The correlation between PSYCOPATHY X1 – X4	X1 – X4
The correlation between PSYCOPATHY and Mean Disapproval is:	-0.17
The correlation between PSYCOPATHY and Culture is:	0.13
The correlation between PSYCOPATHY and Gender is:	-0.01
The correlation between PSYCOPATHY and Professional Experience is:	-0.47

Figure 3.6 Correlation matrix

the correlations between all of the variables in the model. (It is a common practice to show the results in two decimal places.)

The best predictor of psychopathy is professional experience of more than 10 years, followed by culture, then mean disapproval and finally gender has a minor impact. Although this was a small study, it was statistically significant as more than 30 participants took part, who were all professional accountants, which has never been accomplished in the literature.

Overall, the multiple regression for the model is 0.51, which indicates that 51 percent of the variability in the dependent variables (X1–X4) can be explained by the model and X4 or professional experience of more than 10 years is the best explanatory variable of psychopathy. Moreover, neither culture nor gender is a significant explanatory variable of corporate psychopath accountants, suggesting that they are born psychopathic, and they will use the corporate environment to advance their career, as discussed earlier in Section 3.2.1.

In Chapters 4 and 5, we discuss whether blockchain technology or cutting-edge automation or *people-centric* approaches can dampen if not eradicate accounting fraud and curtail the corporate psychopath accountant.

CHAPTER 4

The Promise of Blockchain Technology

Blockchain technology isn't just a more efficient way to settle securities. It will fundamentally change market structures, and maybe even the architecture of the internet itself.

—Abigail Johnson, President and CEO of Fidelity Investments

This chapter explains the fundamentals of blockchain/blockchain technology. The Big 4 firm EY believes that blockchain technology will have the same impact as enterprise resource planning systems have had on the world (**EY 2017**). Since, blockchain technology would increase transparency in the organization and potentially reduce many intermediaries or the human element resulting in a reduction in accounting fraud. KPMG also believes that blockchain technology could be utilized to dampen corporate fraud, as blockchain technology is underpinned by an immutable and transparent structure (**KPMG 2018b**). Consequently, strange or fraudulent transactions can be easily identified as an audit trail will be present. These points will be examined in greater detail and the authors will argue how and why blockchain may serve as an antidote to accounting fraud. Blockchain is underpinned by triple-entry bookkeeping and the discussion will begin with a short history of accounting.

Accounting History

Triple-entry bookkeeping was coined by Grigg (2005) and should not be confused with "momentum accounting" by Ijiri (1986), which is occasionally also referred to as triple-entry bookkeeping. Triple-entry bookkeeping comprises of three entries, the additional entry leading to triple-entry bookkeeping. However, before further elucidating triple-entry bookkeeping, the authors will briefly outline the development of accounting.

It is acknowledged that single-entry bookkeeping or accounting was invented approximately 5,000 years ago in Babylon or modern-day Iraq and is the most basic form of financial recordkeeping. Single-entry bookkeeping is merely a list of assets and debts that are updated accordingly which is suitable for basic tasks but is open to manipulation and prone to errors as there is no authenticate verification of assets and liabilities and method to balance the list.

Double-entry bookkeeping or the Venetian method was documented by the great Friar Fra Luca Pacioli around 1493. It is maintained that this method underpinned the success of Venetian merchants and thereafter became the standard method of recordkeeping business transactions. In double-entry bookkeeping, each transaction produces a *debit* and *credit* event, which cancels each other out ensuring that the balance sheet is in balance. On the other hand, if the balance sheet does balance, there is an error in the double-entry bookkeeping, which can be easily identified by a well-trained bookkeeper, and accounting fraud is harder to undertake. Nevertheless, double-entry bookkeeping is prone to accounting fraud as already discussed in Chapter 1 describing many of the most recent scandals of the 21st century which occur due to fabricated verifications and transactions that allow fraudulent transactions to fall through even robust internal controls. External auditing should theoretically solve the problem of accounting fraud, but its major flaw is that it does not examine for accounting fraud.

Triple-Entry Bookkeeping by Yuji Ijiri

Triple-entry bookkeeping was invented by Yuji Ijiri in 1986 and argued that double-entry bookkeeping records the changes in wealth through the income earned during a period. Hence, in double-entry bookkeeping, changes in balances, such as changes in revenues and cash payments, are recorded. These *events* are documented by two entries,

Debit Receivables	5,000
Credit Revenue	5,000
Trebit: Income Change	5,000

Figure 4.1 Double-entry bookkeeping

namely a debit and a credit, as per on a given date. Whereas, in *momentum accounting* or triple-entry bookkeeping, changes in balances are the known events. Ijiri referred to the concept "the rate at which income is being earned" as "momentum," which is quantified in monetary units per period, such as sterling per month. Moreover, he proposed a third-level entry entitled a *trebit*, which was designed to note alterations in momentum. For example, an increase in credit revenue by $5,000 in a period from $10,000 per month to $15,000 per month would be recorded as shown in Figure 4.1.

Ijiri's triple-entry bookkeeping attempts to create a superior recording system of *momentum* data, which allows for better decision making. On the other hand, it is argued that Ijiri's work was too complex, with little real-world application. The authors believe it is an intellectually stimulating topic but outside the scope of this book.

Triple-Entry Accounting (TEA) by Ian Grigg

Ian Grigg, an expert financial cryptographer, in a working paper, suggested TEA as a method to handle accidental errors or accounting fraud. In essence, he was arguing that companies should not be the exclusive recorders of business transactions and that an external/third party should be the final arbiter. This could be achieved if a cryptographically safe entry was recorded simultaneously when transactions occur between organizations. The third-entry records, the debit recorded by one organization is the credit recorded by the other party. Grigg referred to this new recording method as TEA in contrast to Ijiri's triple-entry bookkeeping or momentum accounting.

	Masud
Debit - Expense	500
Credit - Bank	500

	Joe
Debit - Bank	500
Credit - Revenue	500

Figure 4.2 Double-entry bookkeeping

For example, Masud hires Joe to do some building work. Masud should pay Joe £500, and the double-entry bookkeeping ledger would look as shown in Figure 4.2.

Therefore, the invoice exists in both Masud's and Joe's ledgers: Joe's credit and Masud's debit. In Grigg's TEA, Joe writes a *receipt* on a third shared ledger with a signature. Simultaneously, Masud sees this *receipt*, authorizes, and signs. If such a third entry is recorded unchangeably in a common ledger, neither party can record differently in their own ledger or alter later, that is, no error or accounting fraud is possible as the third entry authenticates this transaction at once. **On the other hand, it is not apparent who would be the trusted and impartial third party that would manage the third shared ledger. However, the advent of Bitcoin underpinned by blockchain technology arose in 2008, indicating that a trusted and nonaligned third party is** *unnecessary,* since the third public ledger as outlined by Grigg (2005) can be "decentralized, immutable, secure, and automated" using blockchain.

Nakamoto (2008) explains that the issue with the current financial system:

The cost of mediation increases transaction costs, limiting the minimum practical transaction size and cutting off the possibility for small casual transactions, and there is a broader cost in the loss of ability to make non-reversible payments for no reversible services. With the possibility of reversal, the need for trust spreads. Merchants must be wary of their customers, hassling them for more information than 10 they would otherwise need. A certain percentage of fraud is accepted as unavoidable. These costs and payment uncertainties can be avoided in person by using physical currency, but no mechanism exists to make payments over a communications channel without a trusted party.

A trustless financial system is evident, since it is a financial system that works without trust, which is possible through the *blockchain*.

Fintech

The exponential rate of growth of technological development is greatly influencing organizations, especially in the financial services industry, resulting in unparalleled opportunities for improvement and innovation. For example, 74 percent of all banks across the United Kingdom expect to eradicate human interaction from their retail banking function within the next decade, and 83 percent acknowledge that they are not supplying the kind of bespoke innovation that digital-savvy customers expect.

Financial innovation can be described as producing and commercializing novel financial instruments/technologies. It takes place in markets and institutions. Cumulative financial innovation, over time, has resulted in the efficient movement of capital and has led to economic growth. Financial innovation can significantly reduce transaction costs, improve security, and potentially lead to superior efficiency. According to a study that utilized data on Italian households' use of debit cards, it suggested that ownership of ATM cards results in benefits worth €17 billion annually to the Italian economy.

On the other hand, fintech delivers disruptive or enhanced innovations to the market, which still utilizes the existing financial infrastructure. The Financial Stability Board (2017) defines fintech as follows:

Fintech is technologically enabled financial innovation that could result in new business models, new applications, new processes, new products, new applications, new processes, new products or new services with associated material effect on financial markets and institutions and the provision of financial services.

Therefore, financial innovation does not necessarily require technology, whereas fintech demands the utilization of technology. Comparison can be made between a credit swap, once a significant financial innovation, which necessitated contractual but not technological innovation, and a digital wallet, which is a fintech innovation.

The capacity of cutting-edge technology, such as machine learning, to capture and process large volumes of data in real time, is significantly changing the way business is being conducted. Consequently, new products and services are being created with the consumer at the center, and fintech is confirming this transformation. It is believed that Australian fintech firms have gained a competitive advantage by exploiting digital technologies, which means that consumers enjoy better *price, convenience, access, choice, and community.*

It can be argued that blockchain technology is also part of the fintech ecosystem, but what exactly is it? In a nutshell, a blockchain is "another type of database for recording transactions—one that is copied to all of the computers in a participating network" (Deloitte 2016, 5). A database needs a central administrator to manage the data/records, which is also permissioned, meaning the administrator assigns privileges or access rights to the users of the database. Whereas a blockchain database does not necessitate a central administrator, users who do not trust each other directly share all records enabling all actors or participants to have a secure copy and observe all changes to the data or records. Therefore, a blockchain database is decentralized, copied, and shared, that is, it is a *distributed ledger.* In a shared or distributed ledger, whenever there is an alteration in the ownership of an asset, the ledger gets automatically revised, and this information is made available to everyone. Consequently, this distributed ledger can support the TEA as proposed by Grigg, where a business transaction between two individuals or organizations can be documented in this third-party public ledger and crucially both parties can *see* this revised ledger. Moreover, as all transactions are recorded in a third-party publicly available ledger auditing and reconciling this distributed ledger becomes redundant.

Blockchain Structure

A blockchain is a collection of records similar to a ledger that is spread across a distributed network of computers which are referred to as nodes. Thus, every computer on the distributed network has access to identical information and crucially operates together to authenticate that the information on the network is accurate. It is important to note that once a transaction on the blockchain has been verified and recorded, it can no longer be changed, that is, the information becomes immutable. In the famous example of Bitcoin, it uses the raw processing power of computers to authenticate the transaction and is called *mining*.

Mining is the production and authentication of the blocks in the blockchain, which are the entries in the blockchain that can be observed by the whole distributed network. However, before a block is appended and permitted onto the network, the information in the block is confirmed by the nodes, and when they achieve a *consensus*, it is added to the blockchain in a sequential order to establish an unbroken record. It is important to note that information in a block can theoretically be anything, products, health records.

As noted, earlier Griggs suggested that a third party should be in control of approving transactions; however, the third ledger is still open to manipulation and cyberattack. On the other hand, the blockchain solves the latter problem because it is entirely decentralized and distributed and above all no single person takes complete control as it will violate *consensus* across the network. **Hence, the blockchain is a trustless and self-regulating financial system.**

Smart Contracts

Smart Contracts were first discussed by Szabo (1994), which is the automation of simple but repetitive tasks or software that monitors conditions and once certain conditions are established then the Smart Contract is executed. Smart Contracts are a bolt-on to blockchains and not part of the blockchain structure. Buterin (2013) suggests that Smart Contracts are "systems which automatically move digital assets according to arbitrary pre-specified rules." Consequently, a Smart Contract could be as simple as paying a supplier or as complex as one that hedges oil prices at a certain price. Consequently, Smart Contracts lead to disintermediation, the process power of transactions is quickened immeasurably, and all are achieved autonomously.

It was also highlighted that Smart Contracts can run autonomous or self-directed organizations also known as decentralized autonomous organization (DAOs). A DAO is completely independent, predicated on Smart Contracts, and requires little human interaction to operate.

The authors **will now highlight the key** blockchain **studies and literature in the context of accounting, auditing, and accounting fraud.**

Accounting on the Blockchain

As explained earlier, blockchain technology is underpinned by TEA, where the three entries are credit, debit, and receipt. Rather than using a trusted third party, the blockchain is utilized. When the transaction occurs on the blockchain, a receipt is created, which is stored on the blockchain and all participants party to the transaction can view it, and if it is a public blockchain, it is visible to everyone.

Deloitte (2016b) explained in an important study that rather than having unique registers for all records everything could be transcribed into blockchain transactions, which would operate as a combined register and would become established as an "interlocking system of enduring accounting records." As these records are cryptographically encrypted, they cannot be manipulated and are open to accounting fraud. Furthermore, the use of blockchain would make transactions more traceable from source to conclusion and save around 50 to 100 working days in attempting reconciliations.

Dai and Vasarhelyi (2017) suggest that blockchain will be the future of accounting as every debit and credit transaction would create a blockchain entry that could be recorded as *token* transfers or *colored coins* between a variety of blockchain accounts. The token contains the complete information of the transaction between the two accounts including the reason for the transfer. Tokenized assets can be virtually anything such as noncurrent assets.

When information has been entered into the blockchain, it can never be changed and be authenticated via the hashes, that is, immutable transactions. On the other hand, if incorrect information is entered into the blockchain it can be altered only after great effort.

It is argued that the blockchain is less likely to be prone to manipulation such as accounting fraud. Since, if a participant attempted to change or eliminate accounting records, they would need to recalculate and authenticate the block. All this is possible; however, it is very expensive, resource-intensive, and observable by other participants in the blockchain. For example, if block 259 were to be manipulated and it is currently block 333, the fraudster would need to recalculate every hash between blocks 259 and 333. If any further blocks were added those too would need to recalculate thereby substantially increasing the workload of the fraudster, that is, blockchain is a great deterrence to accounting fraud.

An important conceptual paper exploring the short- and long-run future of blockchain technology argued that blockchain will be hampered in the short run due to cost, scalability, and technical problems because of vast amounts of data. They suggest that sensitive accounting information could be observable to nonparticipants, which may put off users and damage uptake. On the other hand, even in the short run, Blockchain is an excellent solution for voluntary disclosure and reducing asymmetric information. In the long run, it is argued that blockchain will potentially have a very positive impact on financial reporting as it will help to reduce errors, improve quality, mitigate information asymmetry, and reduce accounting fraud.

Auditing on the Blockchain

An audit is a statutory examination that leads to an opinion as to the truth and fairness of financial statements. Audit, inter alia, involves the examination of a company's revenues, expenditure, review of the robustness and effectiveness of its systems, and compliance with internal and external controls. The economic context has already changed because the internet, coupled with the digital transfer of money or cryptocurrencies through distributed ledgers, is potentially altering the way financial audits are executed. Blockchain is the distributed ledger technology that produces an incorruptible ledger of blocks of information that can theoretically be anything from copyright information to financial transactions. Bitcoin was based on an open-access model so that anyone could possess a copy of the ledger and change it.

It is contended that peer-to-peer networking creates new audit challenges because technology has allowed corporations to cultivate *self-auditing and distributed ledgers that are potentially absolute and self-verifying, thus dampening, if not potentially eradicating, the phenomenon of accounting fraud.*

It is argued that the current model of audit is insufficient to deal with the challenges posed by digital money transfer, storage, and distributed ledger technology. Contemporary audit techniques are not designed to handle the complexity of distributed ledgers, the multiple jurisdiction nature of money/cryptocurrencies, and the time-stamping of transactions. According to ISA 200, which deals with the independent auditor's overall responsibilities when conducting an audit of financial statements, audit risk is the risk that the auditor expresses an inappropriate audit opinion when the financial statements are materially misstated, and in a distributed ledger, this risk is further heightened.

Companies are producing and analyzing ever more data, including that from alternative sources such as social media. *This allows tech-savvy audit professionals to not only consider multiple financial and nonfinancial features of an organization but also provide useful insights, resulting in superior decision making, better quality audits, and, ultimately, greater value for their clients.* At the heart of these changes is the vast amount of data that auditors and antifraud professionals need to utilize. The growing volume of multivariate sources of data, which includes audio, visual, text, and video, demands greater storage capacity.

Mayer-Schönberger and Cukier (2013) refer to a socioeconomic environment where everything can be recorded, quantified, and captured digitally and turned into data, as *datafication*. The result of *datafication* has been the emergence of *Big Data*, a term used to describe large populations of data sets whose size is beyond the scope of regular database software tools to capture, store, manage, and analyze. Big Data is also characterized by specific qualities, termed as the four *Vs*, namely, massive volume or size of the database, high velocity of data added on a continuous basis, large variety of data, and the uncertain veracity of data (IBM 2012). Big Data analytics yields immense opportunities for improvement such as a shift away from *data sampling. Hence, auditor professionals would utilize "all" data sets, including those from comparatively messy data sets, and concentrate on correlation rather than causation, creating a major paradigm shift compared with the current audit process. Since two variables may be correlated such as revenue and receivables, there could be a third factor causing both, which can be established through hypothesis testing which was discussed in the last chapter.*

As mentioned earlier, blockchain is a distributed ledger database that keeps a continuously growing list of transactional records arranged into blocks with various safeguards against manipulation and revision. The potential uses of blockchain are diverse and their effects are so far-reaching that some commentators such as Lansiti and Lakhani (2017) have termed it "foundational technology" because it has the potential to produce new foundations for socioeconomic systems and even "Internet 2.0" (Tapscott and Tapscott 2016). It is even argued that in the future, blockchain technology will lead to complete financial disintermediation.

The threat from blockchain has been acknowledged by many world-class financial institutions such as BNY Mellon, UBS, and the *Big 4* accounting firms, which are heavily investing in blockchain-related projects, even start-ups, to stay ahead of the curve and leverage this emergent technology to their benefit rather becoming a casualty of it.

External audit can be lengthy, costly, and inefficient. Auditors and fraud investigators usually spend their time undertaking repetitive and menial tasks that add little or no value to the process.

Blockchain technology ensures the efficiency and reliability of audit by supplying a real-time, auditable log of ordered evidence of events that are immutable and immediately accessible. When a transaction is recorded in the blockchain and established by subsequent blocks, it becomes a permanent part of the ledger and is accepted as legitimate by all actors in the blockchain network. This will allow easier and faster audit assurance, which will only increase as the technology improves and becomes more widespread. Blockchain technology should allow auditors to automatically verify or authenticate greater sections of the most sensitive data that underpin the financial statements. All these advances are also beneficial to fraud investigators because they can rely on the blockchain-based ledger and focus their effort and resources on the actors and relationships in the blockchain networks as most accounting fraud has an element of management override and collusion. This would significantly drive the cost and time necessary to undertake an audit and fraud investigation without jeopardizing data security or integrity because data would be available only to trusted third parties. Many *Big 4* clients use advanced enterprise resource planning systems, thus enabling auditors to take advantage of Big Data analytics capabilities without being forced to develop new skills.

This benefit is enhanced through partnerships between audit firms, financial institutions, IT firms, Big Data solutions companies, and blockchain initiatives. The following collaborations between the audit profession and stakeholders such as IT companies (e.g., Hyperledger Project and Data Alliance Collaborative) have resulted in reliable analytical tools and open-source blockchain frameworks that will reduce costs.

The quality of audit can be enhanced through blockchain technology and Big Data analytics in several ways. It is suggested that current audit analytical methods occasionally produce many false positive results that cannot be physically investigated by auditors owing to information overload. However, Big Data analytics techniques can significantly reduce the number of false positive results because they identify anomalies and exceptions, along with better systems of ranking, which would also be useful to fraud investigators. Big Data analytics will allow auditors and fraud investigators to look at entire data populations rather than relying on small sample sizes. The data/transactions recorded in blockchain technology are indelible, thereby minimizing the risk of error and preventing data redundancy. In a blockchain system, the integrity of data can be proven rapidly and simply.

It is important to note that the blockchain and Big Data analytics techniques will not dampen the auditor's use of professional judgment and professional skepticism. Instead, an auditor will be able to acquire a multifaceted understanding of the financial reporting system, which should heighten the quality of work and create value for the client (IAASB 2016).

Business risk assessment (of the client) has always been the most important part of the audit process. Thus, 60 percent of participants in a KPMG (2017) study believe that audits should ascertain the client's business risks. The use of Big Data analytics allows auditors to study large data sets more effectively and efficiently, which informs the risk assessment undertaken during the early stages of the audit or investigation, allowing effective planning, especially audit planning (IAASB 2016). It is argued that it is important to exceed minimum compliance standards, and Big Data analytics can make this possible. Blockchain technology is particularly attractive for risk management and compliance when multiple jurisdictions are involved.

It is believed that the following areas will be positively impacted by Big Data analytics and blockchain technology, namely, identifying and ascertaining risks connected with accepting or progressing an audit engagement; detecting and assessing the risks of material misstatement resulting from accounting fraud; identifying and considering the risks of a material misstatement by understanding the organization, including its internal controls; executing substantive analytical techniques based on the auditor's assessment of the risks of material misstatement; and undertaking analytical techniques toward the end of the audit to help the auditor form an overall opinion or the fraud investigator being more confident in their investigation and findings. Therefore, Big Data analytics coupled with blockchain technology gives the auditor and a fraud investigator a more comprehensive picture of the financial reporting system based on bigger data sets and extensive testing in comparison with current practices.

The Risks of Blockchain and Big Data Analytics

As already noted, companies are processing huge amounts of Big Data in terms of volume, velocity, variety, and veracity. However, the seemingly endless data from multiple sources can be of little credible use and unconnected. Therefore, auditors and fraud investigators need to have a concrete understanding of the data they are analyzing and investigating. The following potential data gaps have been identified resulting in the use of Big Data analytics, data consistency, data integrity, data identification, data aggregation, and data confidentiality. These data gaps can cause many audit challenges, for example, auditing data with diverse formats or the identity of actors in the blockchain network.

Analysis of high-volume data sets can result in many outliers for which the auditor or fraud investigator may not have the requisite skills, time, or budget to fully investigate. Another urgent problem is the appropriate identification and adoption of Big Data analytics tools. This problem is compounded by the fact that auditors or investigators may not possess the necessary IT skills to analyze Big Data. This is forcing firms to significantly invest in the right Big Data analytics and attract and retain the best talent. Any operational savings accruing from Big Data analytics and blockchain technology will be offset by higher training costs or investing in data scientists. Notwithstanding the assurance of unalterable, consistent, and distributed databases, blockchain technology faces specific data risks. Although consistency is ensured by the distributed ledger, this creates an expense every time it becomes necessary for a record to be checked with every other record to ensure it is unique, significantly increasing the time necessary to reach an agreement and corroborate the transaction.

In a Big Data world, security and privacy of data from multiple sources received from clients become even more important because a leak can spread almost instantaneously. Organizations that upload their data to a blockchain system or even the cloud are exposed to an unknown or untrustworthy environment, making cybersecurity a major issue. The blockchain system is highly complex, and because audit firms lack IT/IS/data science expertise, they are reliant on Big Data analytics and blockchain third-party vendor solutions, exacerbating security and privacy concerns. The provision of strong data encryption and supply of public and private keys is one possible solution for security issues in the blockchain system. However, this creates another challenge, namely, the loss of private keys. Another significant security risk is the phenomenon of *double spending* that occurs when the data in the blockchain system has been compromised, which increases the chances of further breaches of security.

Although International Standards on Audit state audit practices and there are Computer Assisted Audit Techniques, there is currently no framework for Big Data analytics or blockchain. This highlights the lack of standards or examples of good practice to which auditors or investigators can refer. This will become problematic as different blockchain systems are created and Big Data analytics becomes the norm, leading to protocol problems. Consequently, without a robust framework, auditors are heading into a professional minefield for which they are generally ill-equipped. Auditors will be unable to substantiate their judgments and techniques performed during the audit process. There is also a high risk that International Standards on Auditing (ISAs) do not adequately respond to rapid, constant technological enhancements. In particular, the audit of blockchain technology has received little, if any, attention from audit regulators except a preliminary collaboration between Digital Asset Holdings, a Blockchain-related start-up, and the Australian Securities Exchange. Moreover, 66 percent of respondents in a KPMG (2017) survey comprising chief executive officers, chief financial officers, and chief audit officers of big companies contended that the biggest challenge to enhancing the impact of audit is the regulatory environment. Other threats stemming from the use of advanced technologies are overreliance on data collecting and data analysis software solutions, overconfidence in the results of the performed data analysis, and, consequently, the development of confirmation bias, which negatively affects professional judgment and professional skepticism. In the new blockchain and Big Data analytics-driven world, it is acknowledged that even testing 100 percent of a data population does not suggest that an auditor is able to supply more than a reasonable opinion.

A KPMG (2017) study found that approximately 80 percent of interviewed respondents believed that auditors should utilize higher population samples, and 78 percent believed that auditors should use more cutting-edge IT for data gathering, which is also applicable to fraud investigators. Analysts have highlighted the limitations regarding the processing of information in a Big Data context, such as information overload and information relevance. In a Big Data analytics environment, information can be unstructured, resulting in poor judgments. Another damaging effect of large amounts of data is the tendency of auditors not to ignore irrelevant information. A dangerous effect known as the *dilution effect* can arise whereby higher levels of irrelevant information have been shown to dampen decision makers' ability to identify relevant information (Hodge and Reid 1971). The *dilution effect* is particularly relevant in an audit context because auditors must choose which items are more important for their audit judgments from a large spectrum of information that is equally important to fraud investigators even if they are targeting one area of a financial statement. Therefore, in a Big Data and blockchain world, this becomes even more problematic, and auditors and investigators uncomfortable with the multivariate or unstructured nature of Big Data may avoid ambiguous information, which may result in poor audit opinions or incomplete/flawed investigations.

The FTX Fraud and Blockchain Technology

It is clear from the multibillion-dollar FTX cryptocurrency exchange fraud perpetuated by Sam Bankman-Fried, in late 2022, that blockchain technology still faces challenges. A cryptocurrency exchange platform such as the now defunct FTX is a digital marketplace where users can buy, sell, and trade various cryptocurrencies. These platforms facilitate the conversion of one cryptocurrency into another or traditional fiat currencies like the U.S. dollar or euro.

Unfortunately, FTX had been siphoning customer assets to Alameda, a hedge fund that Bankman-Fried cofounded for use in trading, lending, and investing activities. On November 12, Reuters made the dramatic report that potentially $10 billion in user funds had been transferred from FTX to Alameda. It is important to note that an exchange ultimately makes money from transaction fees on assets that belong to users, a hedge fund like Alameda attempts to profit from actively trading or investing funds it controls.

It remains unclear why those funds were surreptitiously moved to Alameda and when Bankman-Fried first betrayed his depositors' trust. On-chain analysis has established that the bulk of movements from FTX to Alameda took place in late 2021, and bankruptcy filings have revealed that FTX and Alameda lost $3.7 billion in 2021.

On closer examination of Alameda's balance sheet FTX, FTT Tokens were clearly noted. This financial instrument was created by FTX; however, it was not being traded in large volumes in public markets, with FTX and Alameda holding the vast majority. Consequently, these holdings were effectively illiquid, that is, impossible to sell at the open market price. Nonetheless, Bankman-Fried accounted for its value at that fictitious market price.

Disturbingly FTT tokens were actively being used as collateral for loans, including loans of customer funds from FTX to Alameda. This is where the close ties between FTX and Alameda became a blatant conflict of interest: Had they been genuinely independent firms, the FTT token may have been much more difficult or too expensive to use as collateral, thereby minimizing the risk to customer funds.

The utilization of an in-house asset as collateral for loans between secretly linked organizations is like the accounting fraud committed by executives of Enron in the 1990s. In fact, the scale and scope of Bankman-Fried's fraud and embezzlement appear to rival those of Ponzi fraudster Bernie Madoff and Malaysian embezzler Jho Low. The fraud may even surpass larger corporate scandals such as WorldCom and, as already noted, Enron.

Whilst blockchain technology provides enhanced transparency, tamper-proof records, and real-time monitoring of anomalous transactions, it does not eliminate the potential for fraud or prevent security breaches. Fraudulent activities such as the movement of funds in the case of FTX occurred because the exchange was not subject to robust internal controls or superior security measures and crucially external audit such as other more established and reputable exchanges for example Kraken or Bitstamp. Blockchain analysis tools can track and trace funds that go through a cryptocurrency exchange platform to a certain extent. However, their effectiveness may vary depending on factors such as the level of privacy features implemented by a particular cryptocurrency and the availability of data. Certain privacy-centric cryptocurrencies, like Monero or Zcash, utilize advanced cryptographic techniques that make it more challenging to trace the flow of funds. Furthermore, blockchain analysis tools become redundant when funds are mixed or laundered through complex transactions or utilize obfuscation techniques in the case of FTX. Sophisticated fraudsters such as Bankman-Fried may have intentionally hidden the destination of user funds to maintain privacy and collude with Almeda. According to Wright (2022) who spoke to various Blockchain intelligence firms:

> Chainalysis—or any other blockchain analysis tool—can't trace funds through a centralized service because the way that these services store and manage funds deposited by users inherently makes further tracing inaccurate. Even if you could trace through a centralized exchange, *on-chain analysis alone cannot reveal fraudulent intent behind transactions* (Emphasis by authors).

Ultimately, the leaked balance sheet of Alameda triggered global scrutiny and the unraveling of the fraud, and highlighted the importance of strong financial reporting and external audit.

Responding to the Challenges of Blockchain and Big Data Analytics

It is contended that greater adoption of Big Data analytics and blockchain technology will potentially change auditing since audit techniques will become automated, but their scope will widen, resulting in the shortening of professional assignments, which will ultimately improve the general assurance quality. Big Data analytics will probably reduce costs and improve profitability with respect to external auditors/fraud investigators, or cost-effectiveness in the case of internal auditors.

Dai and Vasarhelyi (2016) suggest that blockchain or *mirror world* technologies can facilitate either individual business processes or the entire value chain and can be digitally represented to ensure control and analysis, as demonstrated by projects such as the Hyperledger Project. This system would enable auditors or investigators to use information in the *mirror world* rather than, for example, conducting a physical inventory inspection and supplying sequential integrity assurance. As the *mirror world* or blockchain system documents the details of business activities occurring in the physical world, it can potentially serve as an independent, if not unbiased, information resource to authenticate the veracity of accounting records.

The effective utilization of Big Data analytics and blockchain in audit and fraud investigation requires professionals to improve their skills. In fact, a significant proportion of today's auditors and fraud investigators will need to reskill to fully realize the potential of these technologies. The authors believe that auditors will need to be fully conversant with new technologies but crucially remain ahead of the changes. Furthermore, clients are looking for high information technology/information systems skills, superior interpersonal skills, and critical thinking skills from their auditors and, especially, fraud investigators, who will need to liaise with actors in the Blockchain network. In this regard, PricewaterhouseCoopers LLP, one of the *Big 4* global audit firms that have supported various blockchain projects, has announced a blockchain audit service, which it claims will encourage people to use the nascent technology.

Accounting thinkers caution that with the increased use of Big Data analytics and blockchain auditing, standards must tackle Big Data because the concept of materiality needs to be re-evaluated and the processes producing these data must be constantly improved. However, it is argued that blockchain technology can help lessen the disparity between U.S. Generally Accepted Accounting Principles (GAAP) and International Financial Reporting Standards, eventually leading to a global set of accounting standards that will ultimately dampen accounting fraud.

Given the challenges apparent with the nascent technology of blockchain, it is argued that blockchain technology could be incorporated into Enterprise Resource Planning (ERP) systems. This would ensure an easier transition across an organization using an ERP as only the accounting system would need to be updated. In fact, it is argued that using a cloud-based ERP would be even cheaper to transform and allow the company to quickly reap the benefits of blockchain technology. Hence, the American Institute of Certified Public Accountants (AICPA) and Certified Public Accountant (CPA) Canada are educating their members on the basics of blockchain technology and how it will impact accounting and auditing.

As mentioned earlier, Smart Contract (SC) is a piece of a computer program that can autonomously authenticate, approve, and execute functions given strict protocols. A simple accounting example is paying and receiving inventory; thus, the SC will scan the information, and if the inventory is present, it will automatically issue payment. On the other hand, if the goods received or inventory does not match the purchase order, then payment will not be released. Consequently, the purchase ledger clerk role would transform into a monitoring role. In combination with the blockchain, the SC would be a clear, traceable, and immutable record that could be followed from source to conclusion. SCs can also be employed in complex accounting transactions such as covenant bonds and even hedging the price of oil.

Financial accounting is based on the historical cost convention; however, Blockchain coupled with SCs could potentially allow real-time accounting as SCs could automate significant chunks of accounting underpinned by an immutable ledger leading to arguably the *end of even financial statements*. This would be attractive to organizations that could open their accounting function to important stakeholders, but this may not be suitable for some companies. It is suggested that blockchain may dampen confidentiality, as on a *public blockchain* all accounting information is publicly available although this could be resolved with *private blockchains* and permission rights facilitating limited access.

On the other hand, it is argued that the major deficiency of blockchain is the 51 percent attack. This is possible when a participant on the blockchain controls over 51 percent of the hash rate of the entire network allowing them to begin altering immutable information although this can be mitigated through a permissioned blockchain and already noted earlier would require phenomenal processing power. Worryingly, blockchains cannot differentiate between real and fake information. Consequently, the Big 4 firm Deloitte (2016) has stated that auditors must collect information other than blockchain transactions to arrive at an opinion. For example, if something is purchased and paid for through a cryptocurrency, the transaction is recorded on the blockchain, but an auditor would not be able to establish whether the product was delivered and crucially whether the transaction is legitimate. This violates the whole ethos of blockchain technology, that is, trustless but again *tokenizing transactions could resolve this issue*.

Blockchain technology is still a nascent technology, but the authors believe that TEA has the potential to revolutionize accounting although the time is now to standardize blockchain technology for accounting and audit solutions. The authors believe that the promised benefits and challenges that accrue from the use of Big Data analytics and blockchain/blockchain technology in audit, fraud investigation, and, crucially, prevention, are far-reaching if not groundbreaking. However, all important stakeholders, including legislators, regulators, professional bodies, businesses, and IT developers, need to collaborate if these nascent technologies are to become established in the fabric of global business. It is more than likely that if there is no coherent plan then the business world will witness a breakdown of trust between the audit profession and business, resulting in the unthinkable death of audit and the irrelevance of fraud investigation focusing on accounting fraud. On the other hand, it is acknowledged by the authors that blockchain technology is currently not a universal solution although the Big 4 firms continue to make major investments. Consequently, in the penultimate chapter, the authors will explore alternatives to blockchain technology including automation and *people-centric approaches* such as an ethical and anti-fraud culture to fight and contain the corporate psychopath accountant.

CHAPTER 5

The Halfway House

Automation

> *Automation is driving the decline of banal and repetitive tasks.*
>
> —Amber Rudd, Former Member of British Parliament,
> Work and Pensions Secretary

In this penultimate chapter, the authors will give a brief overview of automation and *people-centric approaches*, and how they can reduce accounting fraud and potentially curb the corporate psychopath accountant.

In previous chapters, we have extensively explored why fraud occurs and the motivations for the perpetrators. According to the fraud triangle, once the *pressure* has been triggered, the fraudster will look for an *opportunity*, which is normally weak poor processes and controls. Ruthless actors usually succeed in exploiting a company's flaws in financial reporting and committing fraud undetected because of inefficiencies, loopholes, a lack of transparency, and poor control management.

Nicodemus (2021) astutely noted "People look at rules, they look at a control, and they say, 'How far can I push this?'." Organizations need to question, what are their people doing to discover ways to break the established protocols and rules?

The 2020 Global Research on Occupational Fraud and Abuse, by the Association of Certified Fraud Examiners (ACFE), examined 2,500 criminal cases from 125 different countries and calculated that the median damages varied according to the kind of fraud. Thus, losses from

fraudulent asset appropriation averaged around $100,000, the corrup-
tion fine was $200,000, and financial statement fraud or accounting
fraud is by far the costliest category of fraud for organizations, resulting
in a median loss of $954k.

So how are these deceitful people able to get away with their decep-
tions? The ACFE (2020) discovered that many frauds used a variety of
nefarious tactics. The most common method of fraudulent coverup was
the production of sham physical documentation (40 percent) followed by
the negative alteration of bona fide physical documentation (36 percent).
This suggests that tangible or actual documentation was used in some
manner in 76 percent of the fraud cases that the investigation exposed. The
study also found that 26 percent of frauds involved concocting electronic
documents and 27 percent involved changing electronic documents.
Finally, 12 percent of the frauds in the study involved no attempt
whatsoever to hide the fraud but were undertaking it covertly.

As stated earlier, the authors will duly give an overview of the
current automation ecosystem, but they argue that automation of an
organizations accounting/financial reporting functions can help identify
and counter fraud in two distinct ways.

First, automation makes it easier and more accurate to complete
regular tasks. Consequently, workers will have greater time to focus their
energies on the dangers/red flags that an organization faces and change
or enhance its processes accordingly. Hence, staff responsible for the
preparation of financial statements and auditors will have more time to
properly evaluate risks and actively search for fraud as they spend less time
manually managing journal entries and reconciliations or other routine
and mundane tasks.

Most organizations give priority to front-end operations such as
developing new point-of-sale systems, more efficient ways to handle
orders, and better way to accept cash and credit cards. On the other
hand, the same attention should be given to the entire finance function
otherwise there will be opportunities to exploit the system.

Second, automation significantly improves workflow effectiveness
since, when year-end financial statements are due or an audit is
underway, organizations frequently encounter a *crunch* of work.

Automation will allow the centralization of data and facilitate greater accountability allowing auditors to use and interrogate the same financial reporting system as the organization operates on a day-to-day basis. This will save time and resources for the external auditor and keep the client engaged. Lastly, automation directs all the information needed for financial reporting into one secure and central location which can be accessed by anybody who requires it or with agreed authorization and access rights. This will minimize fraud and prevent management override which occurs in murky environments with minimal regulatory control over the organization. We will now explore what exactly is audit automation and how it can be achieved.

What Is External Audit Automation?

Auditors today operate in a volatile, uncertain, complex, ambiguous (VUCA) environment that has only exacerbated in a postpandemic world. Hence, more and more auditors are using technology to automate their audit workflow due to vast data sets including swathes of unstructured data such as emails and constantly changing standards.

It is argued that cloud-based audit automation can result in significant improvements in terms of effectiveness, productivity, and security for anything ranging from workpapers to analytics including fraud analytics. Cloud-based technology is utilized in audit automation to give users the freedom to work from any location, communicate with coworkers in real time, and safely access audit data. Consequently, auditors may complete more work in less time with the support of an *end-to-end* online audit solution with seamless data flow between tools.

Why Is Audit Automation Vital?

For audit staff, disparate and insecure applications can lead to version and quality control problems as well as inefficiencies. Aggregating and understanding financial data can be challenging when client accounting information systems are not standardized, resulting in delays and errors that may adversely affect a company's bottom line. We contend that auditors who continue to edit and store audit data using old, on-premises systems potentially risk making their business vulnerable to outdated technology and market forces, that is, if external auditors do not pivot they will lose business.

What Are the Advantages of Audit Automation?

The benefits of audit automation are many and by automating audit workflow, firms will become better at handling typical auditing issues. The following are the principal gains from audit automation:

1. **Real-time collaboration**

   Cloud-based vendor solutions facilitate online audit from any location, underpinned by a system that refreshes your data and stakeholders /client in real time. Thus, allowing audit teams to collaborate on the same document without being concerned about version control and weeding out nonperforming staff.

   With the cloud, there is no longer a requirement for check-out/ sync or backup/restore since, all audit data can be accessible instantly and without any issues. The entire audit team obtains real-time access to the whole engagement from any place due to advanced, multiuser content, trial balance, engagement management, and document retention management. Hence, eliminating the need to transmit, backup, restore, or refresh audit files or move cumbersome files around resulting in security and privacy challenges.

   Furthermore, data from all around the world may be accessed or edited by audit teams, making it simple to plan fieldwork and review procedures across multiple locations and enabling remote staff to communicate in real time. As all staff can observe and have access to the real-time data concurrently, multilocation audits will no longer be a coordination challenge.

2. **Superior Security**

   It is still believed that cloud-based services are less secure than those offered on-premises however, stringent guidelines, protocols, and independent audits, or SOC2 engagements, are deemed essential of cloud organizations. Therefore, Cloud service companies make a substantial effort and investment to adhere to these strict security standards because it is essential to their reputation and not surprisingly financial wellbeing. In addition, by removing critical data from laptops, which are the least secure option, the cloud enhances security and management over it.

It is possible that soon firms may completely do away with manual backups, server upkeep, and software updates by using the cloud. As applications and data are constantly secure and up to date firms can start working by simply signing into a protected web browser.

3. **Data analytics and refining "Auditor Edge"**
   Smarter audit testing, audit data analytics tools, and integrated AI-enabled audit solutions can all help save time and supply your clients with insightful and meaningful information. The most recent technological developments can help in giving clients deeper and more pertinent advice, ranging from audit data visualization to better reporting capabilities.

The traditional audit method used by external audit firms to collect financial and operational data is to choose samples of populations, look for exceptions or outliers, and extrapolate findings for the benefit of their clients. However, innovative data analytics allow auditors to quickly collect client information down to the transactional level, store it safely in the cloud, and run analytics on the information to find risk, including potential fraud analytics. Additionally, auditors can more conveniently and quickly compare the business indicators of their client's industry norms and offer crucial information and guidance to help clients manage their companies more successfully, thus becoming trusted partners rather than a necessary overhead.

As auditing is a very individualized process, each auditor must use significant professional judgment when engaging in decisions including steps like identifying the major audit risks and considering how to produce audit processes to effectively address those risks. Advances in machine learning and other allied technology can help auditors better make decisions. Since it can leverage judgments from thousands of audits to support auditors in real time while protecting client information because audit judgment abilities are often acquired and honed over years of experience, training, and interaction with peers.

The authors argue that by testing complete data sets rather than just samples, supporting risk assessment by identifying irregularities in data, and supplying audit proof through deep analysis of an organization's general ledger systems, data analytics leads to *auditor edge* which facilitates superior audit opinions. Ultimately, the advantages give auditors the chance to continuously learn more about their clients and potentially stay ahead. Automation of audits underpinned by AI-powered technologies can also motivate and empower staff including inexperienced audit employees as they can find solutions quickly and confidently because the audit applications are intuitive, and training can be accessed any time and on any device.

Which Audit Tasks and Workflow Elements Can Be Automated?

An audit is a continuous process; therefore, a cloud-based audit suite with integrated AI-enabled audit software and applications will enable real-time access to audit data, including automatic workpapers, trial balance, and analytics. Auditors will be permitted to request and receive secure online audit confirmations from anywhere in the world due to guided compilation and review methodology, comprehensive data analytics, and value-added customer insight. This will be highlighted in a workflow for an automated audit, beginning with the engagement.

Audit Engagement Management

Engagement workflow will be accelerated by audit automation using a cloud-based organizational center as it provides instant access to all work documents and trial balances in particular:

1. **Workpapers**. With numerous templates, a high level of customization, the capacity to complete multiple jobs at once can be achieved.
2. **Test of balance**. With strong trial balance features such as quick imports, intelligent filtering, and tabling work can be done with ease.
3. **Management of documents**. Standardize and organize large quantities of papers for a project or engagement effortlessly.

The technology allows the entire management of the audit from a central location with full trial balance capabilities, workpaper management, and financial statement reporting functionality, and you can give clients relevant information about the overall status of the work, the status of workpaper signoff, and crucially financial advice.

Audit Methodology

The automation process allows the creation of a bespoke audit program based on recorded risks and assessments using the current risk-based audit technique to avoid overauditing. Specifically, the firm will be able to:

1. **Identify dangers**. Spot any potential hazards in a timely way and examine how other businesses are handling risk in comparable audit engagements.
2. **Succeed peer review**. This will be achieved as the senior managers and engagement partners will be able to rely on audit techniques maintained by skilled editors and authors who make sure the audit programs contents are accurate and up to date.

3. **Save time.** Unique configuration of the audit process will ensure that papers and questions are obtained that you require avoiding duplication and redundancy.

4. **Version control.** As already noted, version control and employee access and authorization problems are resolved in the cloud. It is also possible to incorporate regulatory changes in the field and communicate information while working on engagements concurrently or elsewhere with a trusted engagement process and risk-based architecture.

Secure Confirmations

The automation process allows the secure transmission and online request of confirmations without the requirement for unwieldy and prone to fraud, confirmations from traditional methods. There should be a higher likelihood of a response thanks to a global and simplified network of verified responders. Specifically, the firm will experience:

1. **Automated support.** There will be an automated follow-up on the auditor's behalf ensures a response.

2. **All-inclusive answers.** Audit engagements can be managed from one central location and deliver confirmations.

3. **Security that meets industry norms.** The automation allows the secure transfer of customer account data within a robust system from year to year. Ultimately, audit automation should improve customer satisfaction, reduce costs, enhance productivity, and tackle accounting fraud by expediting the audit confirmation process.

Before we briefly explore the key technologies that ensure audit automation and make the audit function more efficient and effective. The authors believe it is important to reiterate the ways the external audit profession has and will continue to benefit from automation.

Why Audit Automation Is a Workable Solution

Automation allows the auditors to obtain deeper insights and analytics into an organization's operations, study and analyze vast amounts of data using sophisticated analytical tools, and look for fraudulent patterns. This assists in changing the fundamental principle of auditing, which formerly concentrated on the audit of a data sample to **now testing of whole data sets**. This insight allows organizations to explore increasing the frequency of statutory audit or using a continuous audit model so that they are constantly be furnished with potentially value-added operational insights. Thus, the authors believe there in fact be greater demand for assurance services, coverage, faster and cleaner insights, and superior reporting that will increase the organizations' value.

By replacing manual operations with an automated audit system, audit steps are completed more speedily, and fresh insights are continually produced. Resulting in lower organizational expenses, and business operations that are run more effectively.

Auditors can continuously track industry trends and keep an eye on workflows to check high-risk operations. Errors are simple to identify and correct since a continual auditing process maintains uniformity and effectiveness in the results creation process. Hence, error detection becomes more accurate, audit quality rises, and firms produce work of a higher quality.

As the technology facilitates greater speed and ease of processes, auditors should have more time to focus on more complex or specialized tasks that call for discretion, especially on suspicious transactions, and test the validity of judgments such as around revaluation of noncurrent assets. Auditors should be able to deeper and more effective relationships with client teams, raising the standard of assurance reviews, producing additional insights, and making strategic recommendations. The operational effectiveness of the organization increases with the allocation of essential time to such added-value activities.

Before we move to *people-centric*, we will briefly discuss the key technologies that support the automation ecosystem.

Key Automation Technologies

Cloud Technologies

Practically, every industry in the world is touched by cloud technologies in some manner and this was apparent during the global coronavirus pandemic. Since the technology allows the ability to store and access data and programs over the internet instead of on a hard drive. Since organizations usually retain a central data source for the auditors to reference and interrogate, cloud applications allow auditors to access and complete their duties quickly and accurately even remotely. Thereby freeing up time for more constructive dialogue with a client and helping them to make better strategic decisions resulting in a competitive advantage.

On the other hand, auditors must ensure that cloud technologies are sufficient to make the engagement efficient and workable. Consequently, they must pay attention to the speed and agility of such an interface and that it is configured to accommodate any potential future advancements, preventing the need for additional labor during their integration. Given the concerns around the cybersecurity of cloud technologies, auditors must choose the best cloud vendor that can offer efficient risk mitigation techniques to safeguard the highly sensitive data and information stored there.

Robotic Process Automation

Robotic process automation (RPA) utilizes automation technologies to imitate back-office tasks of human workers, such as extracting data and these processes must be repeatable, structured, and governed by rules.

RPA enables the auditors to consider all the audit's processes, redesign any that are ineffective, and rearrange the steps for better outcomes. Hence, the key steps of the audit process including confirmations, reconciliations, email production, and email automation, can be simplified by RPA. Again, freeing up time for more productive contact with a client and helping them to make better strategic decisions resulting in a competitive advantage.

Artificial Intelligence (AI)

To make machines think and function like humans, AI is used to simulate human intelligence in machines. The primary objective is to enable machines to undertake mental functions that people accomplish such as problem solving, decision making, empathy, and other intellectual operations.

The launch of ChatGPT in November 2022 has simulated global interest and speculation about the present and future impact of AI on professional practice. AI has the potential to streamline data collection, analysis, and review, significantly impacting the field of external audit.

The traditional approach to auditing involves analyzing vast amounts of structured and unstructured data. AI is already enabling the automation of specific tasks including data entry and analysis. This will enhance accuracy and speed up the auditing process. AI can generate wider and deeper insights and understanding of complex data sets, which can potentially improve the accuracy and reliability of audit reports. The computerized analysis of accounting transactions is one way AI impacts auditing, detects fraudulent entries, and can raise an alert. AI can process and analyze vast amounts of financial data more efficiently than humans. It can identify patterns, trends, and anomalies in the data, providing auditors with valuable insights. AI-powered analytics tools can assist auditors in identifying potential risks, detecting errors, and uncovering irregularities that may require further investigation.

AI can be utilized to review source documents for example, machine learning tools allow auditors to analyze many contracts in a much shorter timespan in contrast to a traditional manual review. AI can automate repetitive and time-consuming tasks, freeing up auditors' time to focus on more complex and judgment-based activities. Tasks like data gathering, data entry, and reconciliations can be automated, allowing auditors to allocate their efforts toward tasks that require human expertise and critical thinking. Natural language processing (NLP) techniques enable AI systems to understand and analyze textual information, such as contracts, legal documents, and audit reports. AI-powered NLP can help auditors review and extract relevant information from documents quickly, facilitating the audit process. EY (2021) recently reported that:

AI tools have been used to accurately extract information from lease contracts using pre-selected criteria in most cases—a higher level of precision than the average human reviewer is capable of.

One of the most significant areas where AI is accruing major dividends is in risk assessment. Auditors utilize risk assessment to establish which parts of a given client's financial statements are most likely to yield a material misstatement. Consequently, auditors focus more attention and perform more audit procedures on those areas of greatest risk. Traditionally, auditors rely on their experience and professional judgment to identify the riskiest areas of the audit. However, AI can also be used to identify risks that may not have been evident in the past. For example, AI can analyze financial data and identify correlations that auditors may not have previously noticed. This could lead to fresh insights that could improve auditors' understanding of the risks involved in a particular audit engagement.

AI algorithms can identify patterns and anomalies in financial data that may highlight fraudulent activities. By continuously monitoring and analyzing transactional data, AI can flag suspicious transactions, potential compliance issues, or high-risk areas. This enables auditors to prioritize their efforts and conduct more targeted investigations.

It has been reported that ChatGPT can quickly develop an outline of an audit program, which suggests that within a short period of time, AI programs will be able to complete a full-risk assessment based on available data. AI can assess risks associated with specific transactions or financial activities. By analyzing historical data and identifying potential risk factors, AI algorithms can provide auditors with insights into areas that require closer examination, enabling them to focus on high-risk areas during the audit process. AI can aid in monitoring regulatory compliance by continuously analyzing financial data against relevant regulations and standards. It can alert auditors to potential compliance issues, such as noncompliant accounting practices or discrepancies, enabling timely corrective actions to be taken.

AI has the promise to facilitate the concept of continuous auditing. With real-time data analysis and monitoring capabilities, AI can provide ongoing insights into financial transactions and operations, improving transparency and reducing the risk of errors or irregularities going undetected for extended periods.

The question arises will a human still be needed to review the **final** *result?* Absolutely, however, a process that automatically identifies material risks will free up time for auditors to focus on changes required to improve outcomes. AI can significantly enhance external auditing, human auditors remain crucial for critical thinking, professional judgment, and interpreting the results provided by AI systems. The collaboration between AI and auditors can result in more efficient and effective audits and ultimately providing greater assurance to stakeholders.

Predictive Analytics

Predictive analytics is the use of advanced statistical methods where data are used to predict future trends and events. It uses historical data to forecast potential circumstances and produces a list most likely outcomes and the probability associated with them, which can assist in strategic decision making.

Predictive analytics is used by auditors to ascertain patterns in data obtained from the organization they are auditing. These patterns can enable auditors to understand the operational risks, financial risks, operational hazards, and other risks that could affect an organization and make a better assessment of ongoing concerns, which is probably the trickiest part of the audit engagement. Since the auditor will gain an insight into the client organization's likely future condition through comparison with industry data or data from other organizations in similar industries, thereby, raising the quality of the audit.

Collectively, these technologies are part of the ecosystem, which if used properly can make the audit process more scalable, adaptable, and, crucially, *intelligent*, that is, *evolving.* These technologies can investigate data patterns including suspicious or fraudulent, undertake intricate analysis, engage with people, and pivot according to circumstances. Furthermore, these technologies can also automate nonrepetitive, nonstandardized, unstructured, and rule-free procedures, that will produce innovative audit insights enabling savvy auditors to offer a far more lucrative and value-added service and possibly curbing the corporate psychopath accountant.

The authors will now explore *people-centric* approaches that may diminish and potentially curtail the corporate psychopath accountant.

People-Centric Approaches

To be *people-centric* is to put an organization's worker at the center of everything they undertake from sales to day-to-day housekeeping. This approach requires a mini paradigm shift call, which may even require a change in processes, procedures, and protocols especially when it comes to decision making. To become people-centric necessitates a staunch commitment, as it requires buy-in from senior management who probably not be the major beneficiary. **Bitner (2023)** lists the following 21 attributes of a people-centric organization:

1. "Put employees at the center of everything.
2. Deliver great experiences from the beginning. Are you onboarding like a champ?
3. Look for ways to foster connections. Take time to know your people and build relationships.
4. Enable flexible team and work design. Where can you be more flexible?
5. Master communication. It takes 5–7 times for someone to hear and understand a message.
6. Listen to hear and understand. Are you practicing active listening and considering non-verbal signals as well?
7. Pour on genuine gratitude and appreciation. What opportunities are you missing to recognize your people?
8. Resolve conflicts. We know these conversations are difficult, however, resolving conflicts in a timely manner is the best way to build a safe place where everyone feels heard and respected.

9. Include your people in innovative efforts. Don't forget Whirl-pool's mantra, 'Innovation comes from everyone, everywhere.'

10. Inspire your people and build motivation through shared purpose.

11. Minimize ambiguity. Are you being clear and concise? Do your people have a clear understanding of the value they bring to the organization, and how their contributions align with company strategy and goals?

12. Set clear expectations and listen to theirs.

13. Trust your people.

14. Be respectful and inclusive.

15. Demonstrate empathy.

16. Help your people thrive by giving them opportunities to grow and develop.

17. Make sure their well-being is a priority.

18. Make others feel important and valued. Foster a sense of belonging.

19. Acknowledge mistakes. Celebrate learnings and successes.

20. Live the company values. Are you consistently walking the walk?

21. Keep your promises."

Thus, an organization that dares to put its people at the heart of everything it undertakes is an organization that will thrive from the *inside out.* It is acknowledged that the major reputational advantages enjoyed by a people-centric organization are attracting and keeping quality talent and obtaining customer loyalty through enhanced brand reputation, crucially creating high-performance teams, enhancing productivity, reducing staff turnover and absenteeism, generating greater revenue, and becoming industry leaders. This will dampen, if not eradicate, accounting fraud as it will reduce the causes of employee pressure, opportunity, and rationalization or the fraud triangle and even make a corporate psychopath accountant or leader more accountable. The authors will now offer concrete suggestions in the context of fraud prevention.

Accounting Ethics

Ethics is based on substantiated and agreed standards of right and wrong that recommend what humans *should* do, with respect to rights, responsibilities, benefits to society, equity, or specific virtues. It is important to note that being ethical is not the same as adhering to the law. The law often combines ethical standards to which most people will subscribe; however, laws, like feelings, can diverge from what is ethical. For example, the old apartheid laws of present-day South Africa are disturbing examples of laws that radically digress from what is universally ethical.

In the context of professional accounting, which is equally applicable to auditors, the IFAC (2019) dispensed a revised *Code of Ethics for Professional Accountants*. The revised Code highlights a conceptual framework for all professional accountants to ensure compliance with the five basic principles of ethics:

- **"Integrity.**
    - ○ A professional accountant should be straightforward and honest in all professional and business relationships
- **Objectivity**
    - ○ A professional accountant should not allow bias, conflict of interest or undue influence of others.
- **Professional Competence and Due Care**
    - ○ A professional accountant has a continuing duty to maintain professional knowledge and skill at the level required to ensure that a client or employer receives competent professional services based on current developments in practice, legislation and techniques. A professional account-ant should act diligently and in accordance with applica-ble technical and professional standards when providing professional services.
- **Confidentiality**
    - ○ A professional accountant should respect the confidentiality of information acquired because of professional and business relationships and should not disclose any such information

to third parties without proper and specific authority unless there is a legal or professional right or duty to disclose. Confidential information acquired as a result of professional and business relationships should not be used for the personal advantage of the professional accountant or third parties.

- **Professional Behavior**
  - A professional accountant should comply with the relevant laws and regulations and should avoid any action that discredits the profession."

Unfortunately, the five basic ethical principles are not shielded from the corporate psychopath accountant, and accounting fraud is becoming more prevalent due to the ongoing global cost of living crisis. However, the authors argue that it can be minimized if the following 10 principles are actively implemented in the workplace:

1. **Outline clear and strong moral principles.**
   a. An organization's principles, rules, and goal-achieving tactics are all clearly outlined in its written and unwritten ethical standards, setting the tone and direction for the entire organization. This can be further cemented by using a code of conduct or credo, which is an aspirational declaration of the objectives necessary to satisfy the interests of all stakeholder groups. For example, McDonald's (2019) code of ethics is:

   At McDonald's we hold ourselves and conduct our business to high standards of fairness, honesty, and integrity. We are individually accountable and collectively responsible. We take seriously the responsibilities that come with being a leader.

2. **Lead by example and live by the standards.**
   a. If there is no buy-in and adoption from senior management those standards as a guidance for their own behavior, ethical norms and values become redundant and potentially harmful. Thus, it is imperative if not critical for top

management to *walk the walk* when it comes to ethics since, actions speak louder than words especially in the workplace.

3. **Emphasize the importance of organizational standards at key career moments.**
   a. When new hires are employed and current employees are reviewed for performance appraisal, ethical standards must be accentuated. Hence, good behavior should be rewarded if not celebrated.

4. **Utilize meticulous supervision to mitigate for less checks and balances**
   a. Many organizations suffer from deficient internal controls and do not have the budget to employ sophisticated systems to monitor oversight and identify early warning signs of potential accounting fraud. Therefore, rigorous oversight and regular meetings are essential in smaller organizations to ensure clear channels of communication, which may encourage workers to report misbehavior or strange incidents.

5. **Ensure staff take their annual leave**
   a. This keeps staff fresh and gives the opportunity to middle management to assess an employee's work and look for potential fraud. A compulsory vacation policy conveys the message that a staff member cannot work to cover up fraud since, it can and will be detected in their absence.

6. **Establish a cash log, monitor workers who approve payments, and record all transactions.**
   a. When there is a lack of segregation of duties, fraudsters usually target cash. Unfortunately, the entire cash cycle beginning with opening the mail, arranging checks for payment of services, producing a bank deposit slip, going to the bank to deposit the checks, recording, and comparing cash transactions in the ledger to bank statements may all fall under the remit of one worker. Consequently, workers who have the authority to initiate and record payment transactions are subject to rigorous and regular checks and balances.

7. **Consider utilizing experts such as forensic accountants or auditors to periodically review the organization's books and records and accounting information systems.**

   a. Experts such as auditors, can offer deep insights on what can potentially go wrong and suggest improvements to internal controls that will mitigate those risks. They can also evaluate the accuracy of systems and ask challenging questions because of their unbiased perspective.

8. **Create and promote a confidential whistle blowers' hotline.**

   a. The fear of retaliation prevents many workers from reporting ethical dilemmas they are facing. It is possible that workers could also be reluctant to go to their management regarding a coworker out of fear of repercussions and losing face. The creation of a confidential hotline will ensure a robust and relatively cheap reporting system that will ensure timely action and prevention.

9. **Praise good behavior**

   a. Singling out and celebrating ethical and good employee behavior is simple and boosts morale and productivity. However, it must be genuine; otherwise, it will lack efficacy and merely become a tool to promote sycophancy. In contrast, poor and fraudulent behavior must be tackled forthrightly and swiftly or it damages workplace dynamics and breeds even more fraudulent behavior.

10. **Regularly analyze data to identify potentially fraudulent behavior**

   a. Fraudulent transactions leave a distinctive electronic trail or signature in comparison to bona fide organizational activities. For example, they may be processed when no one is looking, at strange hours such as late at night or on weekends, or in unusually large quantities or batches that are slightly beyond approval thresholds. Accountants and auditors have tools at their disposal that can mine data for these anomalies.

It has been stated that *ethical behavior contributes to a successful company*. It is the job of senior management to create an *ethical culture* that will positively impact all behaviors and actions, including relationships with suppliers, customers, employees, shareholders, and creditors, hence, right conduct action should be undertaken for its own sake rather than for the benefit of others. The authors will now explore how this *ethical culture can be fostered*.

Creating an Ethical Culture

The key to creating a robust ethical and anti-fraud culture is the difficult acknowledgment that fraud can happen to any organization and can only be *minimized*. When organizations discover fraud, external stakeholders including the public and the media will probably react negatively, that is, reputational damage. On the other hand, not preventing and recognizing AF is even worse. Early fraud detection can stop further losses, contain increasing negative reputational fallout, and dampen if not eradicate a toxic work environment.

Successful fraud prevention, detection, and reaction are based on organizational cultures constructed on ethical principles, honesty, and transparent accountability. Crafting an ethical culture can inspire all internal stakeholders to play their role in safeguarding the organizational assets and resources including intangible assets such as know-how. As already noted, to create an ethical culture inside an organization, a code of conduct is indispensable, which should be disseminated throughout the organization and deeply rooted into its culture.

All layers of management and personnel are crucial in ensuring an ethical climate in their organizations because in their relevant capacities, they oversee the development and maintenance of a fraud awareness and prevention culture. The authors argue that:

> *Leaders set the climate*
> *Managers uphold culture*
> *Workers determine belonging*

The Nuts and Bolts of Creating an Anti-Fraud Culture

For an organization's anti-fraud efforts to endure and be effective, it is crucial to foster a culture where employees feel empowered and supported to divulge suspicions of fraud. If an organization does not currently have an established or mature anti-fraud culture, then it is prudent to initially gauge what is currently going on and create policies and processes accordingly as a *one-size-fits-all* approach will probably fail.

The authors have developed an anti-fraud culture model entitled the SHEIKH MANIAR ANTI-FRAUD CULTURE BUILDER ("**SM ANTI-FRAUD BUILDER**"), which measures and analyzes an organization's capacity for ongoing progress, determines its stage on the *anti-fraud life cycle*, and identifies processes or activities that may be required to **build** improvement. It is important to note that all models have their limitations, but they are excellent tools for facilitating dialogue and organizational introspection. The SM ANTI-FRAUD BUILDER can be adopted in the following way, beginning by posing the following questions to ascertain the anti-fraud maturity or development of an organization:

- *Does the organization have senior management or leadership buy-in?*
- *To what extent are the current organization's risk management processes known?*
- *How well are the organization's current risk management processes operating?*
- *Does the organization adhere to any external or industry risk management benchmarks?*
- *Does the organization have the capacity to undertake fraud risk assessment workshops, or will it need to subcontract?*
- *Does the organization have the tools, techniques, procedures, and necessary competence to effectively identify, mitigate, and manage the risk of accounting fraud or white-collar fraud in general?*

Table 5.1 Stages of adoption

Negative	• No top-management buy-in • Fraud prevention not a strategic priority including no budget • Anti-fraud only been discussed now in the face of an unfolding scandal i.e., Reactive	• Start fire-fighting beginning with compulsory seminars/workshops for all workers including middle and senior management • Work with PR department to improve communications and proactively deal with negative fallout including social media strategy • Propose a root-branch review of current, if any, risk management policies and procedures • Immediately set up a confidential whistle-blowers hotline • Resistance from senior and middle management • Propose change-management plan
Partial	• Little top-management buy-in • Some awareness of anti-fraud but meagre budget • Anti-fraud only been discussed now in the face of an unfolding scandal i.e., Reactive	• Start fire-fighting beginning with compulsory seminars/workshops for all workers including middle and senior management • Work with PR department to improve communications and proactively deal with negative fallout including social media strategy • Propose a root-branch review of current, if any, risk management policies and procedures Immediately set up a confidential whistle-blowers hotline • Some resistance from senior and middle management Propose change-management plan
Positive	• Genuine buy-in from senior management and open to new ideas • Established policies and procedures including	• Review current fraud risk management policies and processes • Evaluate past organizational frauds and work with PR or Communications Team to review organization comms

(Continued)

Table 5.1 (Continued)

	Whistle-blowers Hotline although dated • Some success in fraud prevention but dealt with internally to avoid reputational damage and sending negative signals to the market	• Hold open and safe workshops with entire staff including senior management discussing the "What, Why, How and Prevention" of white-collar crime • Expand fraud training across the organisation • Celebrate good practice and reward good behaviour • Propose internal and external benchmarking
Take-off	• Strategic buy-in from senior management and open to new ideas • Robust policies and processes • Established KPIs including external benchmarking • Anti-fraud champions across the organisations • Strong anti fraud culture	• Audit current fraud risk management policies and processes including comms • Celebrate good practice and establish a reward structure for good behaviour
Mature	• Permanent buy-in from senior management and across the organization • Good practice and behaviour routinely acknowledged and celebrated • Awarding winning organization for culture and employee satisfaction	• Audit current fraud risk management policies and processes including comms • Celebrate good practice and establish a reward structure for good behaviour • Collaborate with senior management and perform applied research or write a business case study holding out the organisation to be a industry model • Ensure anti-fraud and ethical mindset is part of the recruitment and promotion process for workers to CEO

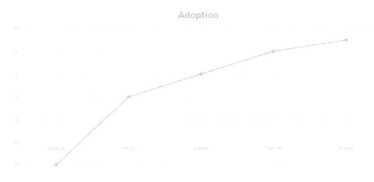

Figure 5.1 Graphical representation of adoption

Table 5.1 lists the stages in the and approaches that should be adopted appropriately facilitate an anti-fraud culture, and Figure 5.1 is a graphical representation.

It should be clear from Table 5.1 and Figure 5.1 that developing a vigorous anti-fraud culture is a journey and requires strategic goodwill from senior management or leadership. Even a mature organization can never rest upon its laurels and best mechanism to ensure anti-fraud continuity is to embed this feature into the recruitment and promotion strategy. This simple intervention will potentially weed out future perpetrators and possibly identify and eject the corporate psychopath accountant at the first hurdle.

We will conclude in the final chapter and summarize key findings from our study.

Conclusion

> *No one can be a great thinker who does not recognize that as a thinker it is his first duty to follow his intellect to whatever conclusions it may lead.*
> —John Stuart Mill—19th Century English Philosopher

Accounting fraud is a special kind of fraud, yet despite its deep negative socioeconomic effects, enhancements in legislation, such as the Sarbanes-Oxley Act of 2002, major improvements in internal controls, and "Many Eyes Are On the Lookout for Fraud," including academics, analysts, and regulators, along with incentivizing the reporting/whistleblowing of accounting fraud through the Frank-Dodds Act 2014, *this phenomenon persists*. According to the Association for Certified Fraud Examiners (2022), in their 12th Edition of their Report to the Nations, the average fraud loss is US$1.8 million dollars. The most prevalent fraud is asset misappropriation, and the most devastating is financial statement manipulation or accounting fraud, which only accounted for 9 percent of cases but resulted in a median loss of $593,000.

Donald Cressey's fraud triangle was extensively discussed and critiqued, which argues that all three conditions "pressure," "opportunity," and "rationalization" must exist for any fraud to be perpetrated. Recent research has highlighted three nonstandard (or deviant) personality types or categories whose behaviors may help explain accounting fraud. These personality types have been designated narcissism, Machiavellianism, and psychopathy or the "dark triad," and it was cited that the psychopathic tendency has a direct effect on the rationalization of the fraud triangle.

Research indicates that senior management contain a greater degree of dark triad personalities in comparison to wider society. It has been hypothesized that the frequency of psychopaths on Wall Street may be higher than 10 percent. If the pervasiveness of corporate psychopaths is so high, then external auditors should incorporate the "dark triad personality risk" feature into their formal risk evaluations and protocols. Auditors remain potentially ill-informed about the incidence of such personality types and, therefore, the greater likelihood of accounting fraud occurring. Thus, there is a need for solutions, such as blockchain technology, to dampen this persistent problem.

The authors successfully undertook an online quantitative study using a variation of the LSRP psychology and associated questionnaire with a robust statistical sample (> 30) of senior audit staff, which was achieved for the first time in the accounting fraud literature. Based on the results, the authors created a multiple regression (Rxy) model that could predict psychopathy or model entitled the corporate psychopath accountant, Y criterion, by using several predictors in combination:

X1—mean disapproval of unethical actions
X2—culture
X3—gender
X4—professional experience of more than 10 years

$$Y = 59.1060 - 2.5840X1 + 0.0336X2 - 0.4386X3 - 7.9113X4$$

The best predictor of psychopathy is the professional experience of more than 10 years, followed by culture, then mean disapproval, and finally, gender has a minor impact. Overall, the multiple regression for the model is 0.51, which indicates that 51 percent of the variability in the dependent variables (X1–X4) can be explained by the model, and X4 or professional experience of more than 10 years is the best explanatory variable of psychopathy. In fact, experienced accountants with more than 10 years' experience may have less psychopathic tendencies suggesting that the corporate psychopath accountant may mellow over time; nevertheless, they remain a high risk for the organization. Moreover, neither culture nor gender are significant explanatory variables of corporate psychopath accountant, suggesting that they are born psychopathic, and they will use the corporate environment to advance their career.

Professional Experience and Its Role in Mitigating Corporate Psychopathy in the Workplace

Corporate psychopathy, as a stable personality trait characterized by manipulativeness, impulsivity, and a lack of empathy, has garnered significant attention in organizational research due to its potential to disrupt workplace harmony and performance. However, professional experience can serve as a moderating factor, as noted previously in this study, shaping the behavioral manifestations of psychopathy through exposure to organizational norms, accountability structures, and developmental opportunities. While psychopathy may not diminish as a trait, its adverse expressions can be mitigated through mechanisms embedded in professional settings.

- **Organizational Socialization and Norm Internalization**
  Professional environments play a critical role in shaping behavior through socialization processes. Ashforth and Saks (1996) demonstrated that structured socialization tactics help individuals align their actions with organizational norms. This alignment often acts as a behavioral check, particularly for individuals with psychopathic tendencies. Exposure to mentorship, training, and collaborative work encourages the internalization of ethical and professional standards, reducing the likelihood of disruptive behaviors. By fostering an environment that values accountability and ethical behavior, organizations can mitigate the adverse impacts of psychopathy.

- **Accountability Structures and Behavioral Regulation**
  Professional settings often impose accountability mechanisms, such as performance evaluations and peer reviews, that deter unethical behaviors. Lerner and Tetlock (1999) highlighted that accountability systems enhance self-regulation by linking actions to tangible consequences. For individuals with psychopathic tendencies, these structures limit opportunities for exploitation and manipulative behavior by promoting transparency and oversight. Professional experience, therefore, enhances an individual's ability to navigate

these systems effectively, aligning their actions with organizational expectations.

- **Development of Emotional Intelligence**
  Another factor influencing the mitigation of psychopathy is the development of emotional intelligence (EI) through professional experience. Goleman (1998) emphasized that individuals with higher EI are more adept at managing interpersonal relationships and navigating social dynamics. For individuals exhibiting psychopathic traits, professional experience often necessitates the development of EI as a compensatory mechanism to maintain relationships and achieve career success. This growth in interpersonal skills helps reduce overtly harmful behaviors and facilitates constructive participation in workplace dynamics.

- **Role Transitions and Maturation**
  Professional experience often coincides with increased responsibilities and role transitions, fostering more mature and prosocial behavior. Roberts et al. (2005) found that as individuals assume leadership roles or manage larger teams, they tend to exhibit greater conscientiousness and agreeableness. These traits counteract the impulsivity and self-serving tendencies associated with psychopathy. By necessitating accountability to team members and stakeholders, role transitions encourage individuals to prioritize collective goals over personal gains.

- **Ethical Training and Leadership Development**
  Ethical training programs and leadership development initiatives are common in professional environments and significantly influence behavioral alignment. Treviño et al. (2006) found that such initiatives enhance ethical decision-making and reduce the likelihood of unethical practices. Regular exposure to these programs helps individuals with psychopathic tendencies operate within ethical boundaries, reinforcing the importance of integrity and accountability in professional settings.

- **Peer Influence and Collaborative Dynamics**
  Workplace dynamics, including mentoring relationships and peer influence, further shape behavior by promoting professional growth and ethical conduct. Kahn and Kram (1994) demonstrated that mentoring relationships provide both guidance and feedback, encouraging alignment with organizational values. For individuals with psychopathic tendencies, this external feedback creates a framework for behavioral adjustment, reducing the expression of manipulative or disruptive tendencies.

The interplay between professional experience and psychopathy highlights the powerful role of organizational structures and developmental opportunities in moderating harmful traits. Through socialization, accountability, and ethical training, professional settings provide an environment where psychopathic tendencies can be managed and redirected toward constructive outcomes. By fostering emotional intelligence, promoting role transitions, and leveraging peer dynamics, organizations create a system of checks and balances that encourage prosocial behavior. While psychopathy may remain a stable personality trait, its expressions in the workplace can be significantly influenced by the cumulative effects of professional experience, as supported by the research of Ashforth and Saks (1996), Lerner and Tetlock (1999), and Goleman (1998), among others.

This nuanced understanding underscores the importance of designing professional environments that prioritize ethical practices, continuous learning, and accountability mechanisms to mitigate the potential adverse effects of psychopathy, fostering more inclusive and productive workplaces.

The authors have argued that blockchain technology can dampen, if not eradicate, accounting fraud. Thus, it is opportune to briefly outline the implications of audit, accounting fraud, and give some hypothetical solutions and benefits for the profession.

It has been established that an audit is a statutory examination that leads to an opinion as to the truth and fairness of financial statements. Audit, inter alia, involves the examination of a company's revenues, expenditure, review of the robustness and effectiveness of its systems, and compliance with internal and external controls. The economic context has already changed because the internet, coupled with the digital transfer of money or cryptocurrencies through distributed ledgers, is potentially altering the way financial audits are executed.

The major criticisms of audit are that the auditing process is a periodic event rather than a continuous cycle. Second, the audit opinion is based on a sampling of entries, amounts, and other information, thus lacking depth and may not detect material misstatements and accounting fraud. Audit standards prescribe that audit evidence should be sufficient, appropriate, and reliable, and generated by specific processes. These processes, for example, confirmations and recalculations/reperformance, are time-consuming and costly.

According to analysts, audit methodology has a major limitation: transactions and accounts are verified or authenticated using sampling, indicating that not all transactions and accounts are substantiated. Consequently, auditors can only give reasonable assurances rather than a complete opinion on the performance of an organization. Blockchain technology can remedy this situation because the transaction data in the blockchain are already authenticated by the transaction parties and crucially sanctioned by the consensus mechanism. The data cannot be manipulated since it is timestamped and hashed, and confirmations will not be required as well; therefore, auditors have the ability and opportunity to verify a complete audit trail. Blockchain also facilitates the continuous auditing of assets such as inventory and liabilities.

If a blockchain network exists between the auditor, the client, and the client's third parties, all of them can have differentiated access to the information. Data are authenticated and sanctioned by the network as it is added; once the information is validated via consensus, this data recognition is unalterable or immutable. As data continue to flow, all network participants or actors can certify and receive real-time updates of transactions, and potentially, a batch process audit may become redundant. As the blockchain supplies automated confirmations of payments, receivables, payables, and inventory, auditors would become capable of scrutinizing 100 percent of the transactions during the consensus process and ultimately giving a superior level of assurance. This would undoubtedly lead to a greater expectation that material errors and the maximum number of frauds, including accounting fraud, should be detected. In addition, the auditor could confirm the viability and design of the blockchain, while checking the network participants or actors and the controls/protocols agreed upon by all. Thus, the auditor would be able to give a much more informed and prescriptive audit opinion, including on the going concern.

Blockchain-enabled auditing augments the efficiency, efficacy, and consistency of the audit evidence collection process—see **Figures C.1 and C.2**.

It is argued that the following features of blockchain technology can potentially moderate the risk of accounting fraud:

- **Security**—Blockchain's disintermediation of data storage thwarts any single participant or actor from stealing company assets. (As noted in Chapter 4, an actor or participant in the blockchain could theoretically take control of 51 percent, but this would require phenomenal processing power, and alterations to the hash keys would be challenging, as previous ones would also need to be changed. Even if a change is made, all actors in the blockchain could see the attack and take remedial action, such as closing access to their part of the blockchain network. Furthermore, the authors believe that as

Audit Framework	Current Methods / Protocols	Blockchain-Enabled Audit
Analytical Procedures	Statistical operations	Perform real time data analysis: descriptive, predictive, and prescriptive
Observation and inquiry	Written or oral / interview enquiry	Inspect Blockchain and information flow including access and rights to information
Testing of calculations	Probe Accounting Information System and perform recalculations and reperforming process flows	Scrutinise Blockchain including inputs / hash keys and information flow including access and rights to information Identify any anomalies or outliers
Physical verification of source documentation / records and non-current assets	Sampling, walk through tests, verification / tracing / matching	Analyse Blockchain including inputs / hash keys and information flow including access and rights to information
Confirmation	Verify balances	Examine Blockchain and information flow

Figure C.1 Blockchain impact on the audit framework

Accounting Process	Current practice	Blockchain solution
Closing periods and year ends	Time consuming procedures ensuring cut off	There is cut off in Blockchain and vendor solutions allow production of fast, authenticated and efficient financial statements and dash boards
Internal and external reporting	Time consuming tests that authenticate information	See above and allows accountants to offer more value-added services such as management consulting and advice
Reconciliation of accounts	The boring and overwhelming act of comparing internal documentation with external documentation	Blockchain facilitates efficient and streamlined processes and information which is agreed by all stakeholders in the

Figure C.2 Blockchain effect on accounting processes

blockchain technology continuously improves and becomes ubiquitous, it will be more secure, and potentially, 100 percent control will be required to execute any fraud.)

- **Integrity**—Blockchain's structure creates a certifiable record of every transaction that has been made, which can only be produced and/or changed with consensus.
- **Traceability**—Blockchain's irrevocability and immutability assign an enduring, time-stamped audit trail for every phase of a business transaction and/or process.
- **Transparency**—Blockchain's decentralized network supports a clear platform in which fraudulent information and transactions can be easily identified, investigated, and reported.

The following are well-documented and notorious billion-dollar examples of financial fraud where blockchain technology could have been used to limit the magnitude of the fallout if not stop them.

Bernard Madoff was imprisoned for securities fraud in 2009, having masterminded a Ponzi or pyramid investment scheme whereby primary investors withdrew money (fraudulently classified as profits) at the expense of new participants. It was reported that investors lost up to $65 billion dollars. It is argued that if blockchain smart contracts had been available and utilized at the time, there could have been superior internal and external audibility and transparency of the fund, which would have been underpinned by preprogrammed rules and protocols written in permanent code that would strictly be followed by the active nodes. Meaning that the assets could only be invested according to those predetermined rules, hence making it virtually impossible to claim ownership or disposal of an asset that violated the established rules, that is no management override.

In the case of Enron, the now-defunct external auditor Arthur Anderson was supposed to authenticate the financial statements and give assurances to their stakeholders. Unfortunately, the firm was found guilty of hindering justice after shredding thousands of audit documents and files. Utilizing blockchain technology and smart contracts, the auditing process becomes cheaper, faster, and more transparent. If the data had been recorded to a public ledger/blockchain, the transactions would have been clearly visible to all participants, and any accounting fraud would have been detected. Even if a permissioned network had been in operation, the company/Enron could constrain the participants and their access rights. Thus, specific participants would be supplied with cryptographic identity cards to enable viewing of all or limited transactions. On the other hand, even such prioritized users would be unable to modify the blockchain without consensus, suggesting that most participants would need to collaborate to commit fraud.

In both cases, the encrypted information would remain permanent and all participants clearly perceptible, meaning anyone attempting to commit a fraud would be visible.

There are potential "win-win" benefits for the accountant and their client as outlined in **Figure C.3.**

The authors believe that the case for blockchain technology to facilitate the reduction if not the elimination of accounting fraud is robust and established. Consequently, the authors took the liberty of talking to subject matter experts and current auditors to gauge their perceptions of blockchain technology and found the following:

- As blockchain diminishes the human element, then accounting fraud should significantly fall and stop the corporate psychopath accountant from wreaking havoc.

Blockchain Feature	Accountant Benefit	Client Benefit
Real time supply of information	Ability to undertake real time analytical reviews / procedures	Robust and accurate information available in real time
Authentication of data by network actors	Noticeably less time spent confirming and verifying information	Less time spent chasing outstanding balances and resolving issues
Various levels or degrees of access	Access to Blockchain and potential for continuous audit	Ability to add users with differentiated access on the Blockchain

Figure C.3 Benefits of blockchain to the accountancy profession

- Suspicious management override should become nonexistent.
- Audit assurance should increase, and going concern statements should become prescriptive, allowing superior recommendations.
- Efficient and cheaper external audit allows firms to offer other services.
- The nature of external audit changes and supplies assurance over the validity of transactions.
- SCs will create financial dis-intermediation leading to a major reduction in third-party intermediaries including lawyers.
- As the information on the blockchain is immutable and cannot be erased, the transfer of ownership rights will become highly transparent.
- Blockchain technology is decentralized, ensuring no one owns the information either in a public or closed blockchain. Thus, there will no longer be a need for the information to be aggregated and warehoused in central databases, as it will be stored everywhere at once.
- The biggest challenges to the adoption of blockchain will be cost and training.
- Small- and medium-sized practices will probably wait until the technology becomes ubiquitous.

It is estimated that by 2024, the global blockchain market will be worth $20 billion, and the migration to a financial system predicated on blockchain technology offers multiple opportunities for the profession. Since accountants are perceived as experts in record keeping, application of complex rules, business planning, and standards setting, and auditors are specialists in giving assurance to stakeholders. They have a golden opportunity to guide and influence how blockchain is implanted and utilized in the future, and above all, to create cutting-edge blockchain-led solutions and services. Ultimately to become a genuinely fundamental part of the global financial ecosystem, blockchain must be cultivated, harmonized, and augmented. This is a lengthy process that may take another decade; however, whoever takes the initiative and crucially invests in the right human capital will reap the greatest operational and financial harvest. Nevertheless, the authors believe that automation and "people-centric" approaches, which were extensively explored in Chapter 5, are necessary preparations until blockchain technology becomes universal and fully functional. The authors contend that automating an organization's accounting and financial reporting processes can aid in two different ways in identifying and combating fraud.

First off, automation streamlines and improves the accuracy of routine processes. As a result, employees will have more time to concentrate on the risks or warning signs that an organization faces and adjust or improve its processes as necessary. As a result, staff members in charge of preparing financial statements and auditors will have more time to appropriately assess risks and actively look for fraud because they will spend less time manually managing journal entries, reconciliations, and other mundane processes.

Second, automation makes it easier and more accurate to complete regular tasks. Consequently, workers will have greater time to focus their energies on the dangers/red flags that an organization faces and change or enhance its processes accordingly. Hence, staff responsible for the preparation of financial statements and auditors will have more time to properly evaluate risks and actively search for fraud as they spend less time manually managing journal entries and reconciliations or other routine and mundane tasks. Most businesses prioritize front-end tasks like creating new point-of-sale systems, handling orders more effectively, and improving how they collect cash and credit cards. On the other hand, the same attention should be given to the entire finance function otherwise there will be opportunities to exploit the system.

Automation also greatly increases workflow efficiency since organizations commonly experience a "crunch" of work when year-end financial statements are due, or an audit is underway. Automation will enable data centralization and increased accountability by enabling auditors to access and query the same financial reporting system that the organization uses daily. The external auditor will benefit from time and resource savings, and the customer will remain engaged. Finally, automation consolidates all the data required for financial reporting into a single, safe area that is accessible to anybody who needs it or has been granted authorization and access privileges. By doing this, accounting fraud will be reduced and management override—which happens when there is little regulatory oversight of the organization—will be avoided.

A genuine "people-centric" strategy that can reduce accounting fraud is founded on several aspects that were thoroughly discussed in Chapter 5. The SHEIKH MANIAR ANTI-FRAUD CULTURE BUILDER (also known as the "SM ANTI-FRAUD CULTURE BUILDER") is an anti-fraud culture model created by the authors. It assesses an organization's capacity for continuous improvement, as well as its stage in the "anti-fraud life cycle" and the potential processes or activities needed to "build" improvement.

The authors believe that until blockchain technology becomes established and a viable option for most organizations, automation and "people-centric" approaches are the optimal ways to minimize accounting fraud and, ultimately, curb the influence of the corporate psychopath accountant or charm the "corporate snake," who will continue to lurk as an organizational dark shadow. Consequently, organizations must remain vigilant, and in the words of *Rum (A 12th-century metaphysician and poet par excellence):*

The snake is your animal-soul. When you bring it into the hot air of your wanting-energy, warmed by that and by the prospect of power and wealth, it does massive damage.

Glossary

ACCA: Association of Chartered Certified Accountants.

Accounting: Is the discipline or identifying, recording, analyzing transactions, communicating financial statements, and informing decision making.

Accounting Ethics: These ensure integrity, impartiality, and accountability in financial reporting and business practices and refer to the principles, beliefs, and standards that direct ethical behavior and decision making in the accounting profession.

AICPA: American Institute of Certified Public Accountants.

Accounting Fraud: See Financial Statement Fraud.

Agency Theory: Examines how principals (like shareholders) and agents (like managers) interact, and how their divergent interests, can be better aligned using accounting data.

Anti-Fraud Controls: These are internal policies, procedures, and checks that businesses use to stop, detect, and discourage (accounting) fraud.

Artificial Intelligence: Refers to the incorporation of clever algorithms and technologies into blockchain systems to improve skills like data analysis, automation, and decision making, creating new opportunities for decentralized applications.

Asset Misappropriation: The theft or improper use of an entity's assets, frequently carried out by workers or those in positions of trust.

Assets: Financial resources that a company owns and is anticipated to use in the future.

Audit: An unbiased investigation and confirmation of a business's financial records, transactions, and internal controls to confirm accuracy and conformity with statutory requirements.

Audit Trail: A record that shows how accounting transactions were carried out in order from their inception to the final financial statement.

Automation: This is the use of technology and systems to carry out operations with little to no human involvement, hence boosting productivity, efficiency, and accuracy.

Balance Sheet (Statement of Financial Position): A financial statement that gives a quick overview of a company's financial situation at a certain period by listing its assets, liabilities, and equity.

Bankruptcy: A legal procedure in which people or businesses declare they are unable to pay their obligations and seek to be protected from creditors.

Blockchain Technology: This is a decentralized, open-source digital ledger that securely logs transactions and confirms them across numerous computers. This ensures immutability and fosters confidence across a variety of businesses.

Cloud Technology: This is an umbrella term where users can access and use resources remotely and on-demand. This includes computing services like storage, processing power, and software programs.

Collusion: A covert agreement or plan between two or more people to cheat or deceive others.

Concealment: This is the act of concealing or hiding information or assets to avoid detection or to deceive others.

Corporate Culture: Shared values, beliefs, attitudes, and behaviors inside an organization that influence its overall environment and atmosphere.

Corporate Fraud: Unlawful actions taken by someone working for a firm to defraud stakeholders, investors, or shareholders, frequently including senior management or staff.

Credit: An entry on the right side of an account that lowers assets and expenses while raising liabilities and equity.

C R I M E Model: This model comprises *"Cooks," "Recipes," "Incentives," "Monitoring," and "End results"* that explain the causes and effects of Accounting Fraud.

Dark Triad: The three personality qualities narcissism, Machiavellianism, and psychopathy are collectively referred to as the "dark triad." People that exhibit the dark triad characteristics frequently lack compassion and morality and engage in manipulative, exploitative, and antisocial behaviors.

Data Analytics: This is the act of poring over vast amounts of data to find trends, connections, and insights that might aid in decision making or spot abnormalities.

Debit: An entry on the left side of an account that lowers obligations, equity, and revenues while raising assets and expenses.

Double-Entry Accounting: A method of recording financial transactions that necessitates equal debits and credits in order to uphold the accounting formula (assets = liabilities + equity).

Embezzlement: Fraudulently taking possession of money or property entrusted to someone else's care, usually by an employee or fiduciary.

Equity: The remaining stake in a company's assets after liabilities are subtracted. It stands for the claim of the owner or shareholders to the company's resources.

Expenses: These are the costs a business incurs to produce income, such as employee salaries, rent, or utility charges.

Financial Reporting: This is the process of documenting and communicating an organization's financial performance and position through statements, disclosures, and presentations.

Financial Statement Fraud: When financial statements are purposefully manipulated or misrepresented to fool users and give them a false impression of the state of the business.

Fraud: Intentional deception or misrepresentation that benefits the perpetrator at the expense of another party and results in financial or personal gain.

Fraud Diamond Model: This model is an expansion of the fraud triangle theory and adds the concept of capability to the triangle's three components.

Fraud Examination: A methodical procedure for obtaining, examining, and recording evidence to find fraudulent actions; frequently involves conducting interviews, reviewing documents, and analyzing data.

Fraud Pentagon Model: The model extends the fraud triangle theory by adding the variables of capacity and collusion.

Fraud Scale Model: This model classifies fraud schemes according to their impact and level of sophistication ranging from small-scale staff embezzlement to accounting fraud.

Fraud Triangle Theory: This theory describes how pressure, opportunity, and rationalization all contribute to fraudulent behavior.

Fraudulent Financial Reporting: See Financial Statement Fraud.

Generally Accepted Accounting Principles (GAAP): These maintain uniformity and consistency in financial reporting.

Going Concern: The presumption that a company will carry on operating indefinitely absent evidence to the contrary, which has an impact on the valuation and presentation of assets and liabilities.

Internal Controls: Measures taken by a company to protect its resources, assure the correctness of its financial data, and thwart fraud and mistakes.

International Financial Reporting Standards (IFRS): These are a collection of accounting guidelines and standards that are applied globally to ensure the comparability and uniformity of financial reporting.

Liabilities: A company entity's debts or obligations that call for future resources or payments.

Machiavellianism: A personality feature characterized by cunning, deceit, and a readiness to take advantage of others.

MICE Model: According to the MICE fraud hypothesis, there are four main motivations for people to commit fraud: monetary gain, ideological conviction, coercion, and ego.

Mining: The practice of validating and adding new transactions to the blockchain by solving challenging computational puzzles, frequently requiring the use of specialized hardware, in exchange for benefits or incentives is referred to as mining in the context of blockchain.

Multiple Regression Model: A statistical analysis that examines the relationship between a dependent variable and two or more independent variables. By evaluating the size and direction of each factor's effect while taking other variables into consideration, it enables researchers to ascertain how several factors collectively affect the outcome of interest. The model aids in making predictions or describing fluctuations in the dependent variable by shedding light on how various factors interact simultaneously.

Narcissism: A psychological trait characterized by an exaggerated feeling of one's own importance, a persistent desire for adulation, and a lack of empathy for others.

Predictive Analytics: This is the process of using patterns, trends, and insights to forecast future results and make educated predictions about upcoming events or behaviors.

Profit and Loss Statement (Income Statement): A financial statement used to calculate a company's net income or net loss by compiling a summary of its revenues, costs, profits, and losses for a given period.

Psychopath: This is a person who consistently engages in antisocial behavior, without empathy or regret, has manipulative tendencies, and has no regard for other people's rights or social conventions. They might have charming or charismatic qualities, but they don't have real emotional connections or care about other people's well-being.

Psychopathy: A personality attribute characterized by impulsivity, antisocial behavior, lack of regret or empathy, and a propensity for dishonest or manipulative behavior.

Revenue: The money a business makes from doing business, such as selling products or services.

Robotic Process Automation: RPA includes simulating human interactions with computer systems by utilizing software robots or bots to automate routine, rule-based processes.

Sarbanes-Oxley Act (SOX): This is a federal law in the United States that was passed to improve the internal control, financial reporting, and corporate governance standards for publicly traded businesses.

Smart Contracts: These are self-executing digital agreements that automatically enforce and enable a contract's terms and conditions without the need for intermediaries, offering efficiency, transparency, and security.

Whistle-blower: A person who brings attention to or reveals fraudulent, unlawful, or unethical activity within an organization.

White-Collar Crime: Nonviolent crimes frequently committed by people in office or corporate settings and frequently involving monetary or economic considerations.

References

ACCA. 2017. "Auditors Get to Grips with New Challenges." Accessed December 22, 2017. www.accaglobal.com/uk/en/member/member/accountingbusiness/2017/01/insights/audit-challenges.html.

ACFE. 2014. "Report to the Nations on Occupational Fraud and Abuse." *Global Fraud Study*. Accessed January 1, 2019. www.acfe.com.

ACFE. 2016. "Report to the Nations on Occupational Fraud and Abuse." *Global Fraud Study*. Accessed January 1, 2019. www.acfe.com.

ACFE. 2018. "Report to the Nations on Occupational Fraud and Abuse," *Global Fraud Study*. Accessed February 1, 2020. www.acfe.com.

ACFE. 2019. "Report to the Nations on Occupational Fraud and Abuse." *Global Fraud Study*. www.acfe.com.

ACFE. 2020. "Report to the Nations on Occupational Fraud and Abuse." *Global Fraud Study*. www.acfe.com.

ACFE. 2021. "Report to the Nations on Occupational Fraud and Abuse." *Global Fraud Study*. www.acfe.com.

ACFE. 2022. "Report to the Nations on Occupational Fraud and Abuse." *Global Fraud Study*. www.acfe.com.

AICPA. 2005. *Management Override of Internal Controls: The Achilles' Heel of Fraud Prevention*. New York: AICPA.

AICPA. 2021. "Consideration of Fraud in a Financial Statement Audit." https://us.aicpa.org/content/dam/aicpa/research/standards/auditattest/downloadabledocuments/au-c-00240.pdf.

Albrecht, C., C. Turnbull, Y. Zhang, and C.J. Skousen. 2010. "The Relationship Between South Korean Chaebols and Fraud." *Managerial Auditing Journal* 33(3): 257–268.

Albrecht, C., C.C. Albrecht, and S. Dolan. 2007. "Financial Fraud: The How and Why." *European Business Forum* (29): 34–39.

Albrecht, C.C., W.S. Albrecht, and C.O. Albrecht. 2008. *Fraud Examination*. Cengage Learning.

Albrecht, S., K. Howe, and M. Romney. 1984. "Deterring Fraud: The Internal Auditor's Perspective." *Institute of Internal Auditors Research Foundation* 3(3): 1–42.

Albrecht, W.S. 2006. *Fraudulent Financial Transactions*. PhD Thesis. Brigham: Brigham Young University. Accessed March 1, 2019. www.aicpa.org/Pages/default.aspx.

Albrecht, W.S. 2014a. "My Reflections on How the ACFE Began." *Fraud Magazine*, May/June 2014.

Albrecht, W.S. 2014b. "Iconic Fraud Triangle Endures: Metaphor Diagram Helps Everybody Understand Fraud." *Fraud Magazine*, May/June 2014. Accessed online April 2019. www.fraud-magazine.com/article.aspx?id=4294983342.

Albrecht, W.S., and C.C. Albrecht. 2002. "Root Out Financial Deception." *Journal of Accountancy* 193(4): 30–36.

Albrecht, W.S., C. Albrecht, and C.C. Albrecht. 2008. "Current Trends in Fraud and Its Detection." *Information Security Journal: A Global Perspective* 17(1): 2–12.

Albrecht, W.S., C.C. Albrecht, and C.O. Albrecht. 2004. "Fraud and Corporate Executives: Agency, Stewardship and Broken Trust." *Journal of Forensic Accounting* 5(1): 109–30.

Albrecht, W.S., G. Wernz, and T. Williams. 1995. *Fraud: Bringing Light to the Dark Side of Business*. 1st ed. New York: McGraw-Hill.

American Institute of Certified Public Accountants (AICPA). 2021. *Consideration of Fraud in a Financial Statement Audit (AU-C Section 240)*.

Anderson, J.R., and M. Tirrell. 2004. "Too Good to be True: CEOs and Financial Reporting Fraud." *Consulting Psychology Journal: Practice and Research* 56: 35–43.

Andrews, H., and P. Furniss. 2009. "A Successful Leader or a Psychopathic Individual?." *Management Services*, 53(4): 22–24.

Appelbaum, D., and R. Nehmer 2017. "Designing and Auditing Accounting Systems Based on Blockchain and Distributed Ledger Principles." Feliciano School of Business.

Arjoon, S. 2005. "Corporate Governance: An Ethical Perspective." *Journal of Business Ethics* 61(4): 343–52.

Ashforth, B. E., and A.M. Saks. 1996. "Socialization Tactics: Longitudinal Effects on Newcomer Adjustment." *Academy of Management Journal* 39(1): 149–78. https://doi.org/10.2307/256634.

Babiak, P., and R.D. Hare. 2019. *Snakes in Suits: When Psychopaths Go to Work*. Harper Collins.

Babiak, P. 2007. "From Darkness into the Light: Psychopathy in Industrial and Organizational Psychology." In *The psychopath: Theory, research, and practice*, edited by H. Herve' and J.C. Yuille (pp. 411–28). Mahwah, NJ: Erlbaum.

Babiak, P., and M.E. O'Toole. November 2012. "The Corporate Psychopath," *FBI Law Enforcement Bulletin*. Accessed December 26, 2017. www.fbi.gov/stats services/publications/lawenforcement-bulletin/november-2012/the-corporate-psychopath.

Babiak, P., C.S. Neumann, and R.D. Hare. 2010. "Corporate Psychopathy: Talking the Walk." *Behavioural Sciences and the Law* 28: 174–93.

Bailey, C. 2015. "Psychopathy and Accounting Students' Attitudes towards Unethical Professional Practices."

Bailey, C. 2017. "Psychopathy and Accounting Students' Attitudes towards Unethical Professional Practices." *Journal of Accounting Education* 41: 15–32.

Baofu, P. 2014. *The Future of Post Human Accounting: Towards a New Theory of Addition and Subtraction in Information Management.* IAP. Charlotte, North Carolina (NC)

BBC. 2003. "Parmalat in Bankruptcy Protection." http://news.bbc.co.uk/1/hi/business/3345735.stm.

BBC. 2004. "New Detention in Parmalat Probe." Accessed November 22, 2018. http://news.bbc.co.uk/2/hi/business/3487192.stm.

Beasley, M. 1999. "An Empirical Analysis of the Relationship between the Board of Directors' Composition and Financial Statement Fraud." *The Accounting Review* 71(4): 443–65.

Beasley, M.S., J.V. Carcello, and D.R. Hermanson. 1999. "Fraudulent Financial Reporting: 1987–1997, An Analysis of U.S. Public Companies." *Committee of Sponsored Organisations of the Treadway Commission.* Accessed January 1, 2019. www.coso.org.

Beasley, M.S., J.V. Carcello, D.R. Hermanson, and T.L. Neal. 2010. "Fraudulent Financial Reporting 1998–2007: An Analysis of U.S. Public Companies." *Committee of Sponsored Organisations of the Treadway Commission.* Accessed March 1, 2019. www.coso.org.

Beasley, M.S., V.J. Carcello, and D.R. Hermanson. 2000. "Preventing Fraudulent Financial Reporting." *The CPA Journal* 70(12): 15–21.

Bierstaker, J.L., G.R. Brody, and C. Pacini. 2006. "Accountants' Perceptions Regarding Fraud Detection and Prevention Methods." *Managerial Auditing Journal* 21(5): 520–35.

Bitner. 2023. "What Does it Mean to Be people-Centric?21 Signs Your Organization Has a People-Centric Culture." *Centricity.* www.centricitynow.com.

Bloomberg. 2004. "Bloomberg Businessweek." Accessed January 1, 2019. www.bloomberg.com/news/articles/2004-01-11/how-parmalat-went-sour.

Boddy, C.R.P. 2010. "Corporate Psychopaths and Organizational Type." *Journal of Contemporary Affairs* 10(4): 300–312.

Brinkley, C.A., W.A. Schmitt, S.S. Smith, J.P. Newman. 2000. "Construct Validation of a Self-Report Psychopathy Scale: Does Levenson's Self-Report Psychopathy Scale Measure the Same Constructs as Hare's Psychopathy Checklist-Revised?" 31(7): 1025.

Brown-Liburd, H., and A.M. Vasarhelyi. 2015. "Big Data and Audit Evidence." *Journal of Emerging Technologies in Accounting* 12(1): 1–16.

Brown-Liburd, H., H. Issa, and D. Lombardi. 2015. "Behavioural Implications of Big Data's Impact on Audit Judgment and Decision Making and Future Research Directions." *Accounting Horizons* 29(2): 451–68.

Buterin, V. 2013. "A Next Generation Smart Contract & Decentralized Application." Accessed August, 2021. www.weusecoins.com/assets/pdf/library/Ethereum_white_paper_a_next_generation_smart_contract_and_decentralized_application_platform_vitalik-buterin.pdf.

Capgemini. 2017. "The Fintech Advantage: Harnessing Digital Technology, Keeping the Customer in Focus." The_fintech_advantage.pdf (www.capgemini.com).

CCN. 2018. "Big Four Giant PwC Announces Blockchain Auditing Service." Accessed May 20, 2018. www.ccn.com/pwc-to-provide-audit-service-for-blockchain-to-stimulate-adoption/.

Centre for Audit Quality. December 2010. "Deterring and Detecting Financial Reporting Fraud: A Platform for Action." 1–32. Accessed January 1, 2019. www.aicpa.com.

Choo, F., and K. Tan. 2007. "An 'American dream' Theory of Corporate Executive Fraud." *Accounting Forum* 31: 203–15.

Cielswicz, J.K. 2012. "The Fraud Model in International Contexts: A Call to Include Societal-Level Influences in the Model." *Journal of Forensic and Investigative Accounting* 4(2): 214–54.

CNBC. 2020. "The Enron of Germany: Wirecard Candal Casts a Shadow on Corporate Governance." www.cnbc.com/2020/06/29/enron-of-germany-wirecard-scandal-casts-a-shadow-on-governance.html.

Cohen, J., Y. Ding, C. Lesage, and H. Stolowy. 2010. "Corporate Fraud and Managers' Behaviour: Evidence from the Press." *Journal of Business Ethics* 95: 271–315.

Courtois, C., and Gendron, Y. 2017. "The 'Normalization' of Deviance: A Case Study on the Process Underlying the Adoption of Deviant Behaviour." *Auditing: A Journal of Practice & Theory* 36(3):15–43.

Cressey, D. 1973. *Other People's Money*. Montclair, NJ: Patterson Smith.

Cressey, D.R. 1950. "The Criminal Violation of Trust." *American Sociological Review* 15(6): 738–40.

Cressey, D.R. 1953. *Other People's Money: A Study in the Social Psychology of Embezzlement*. Glencoe: The Free Press.

Dai, J., and M.A. Vasarhelyi. 2016. "Imagineering Audit 4.0." *Journal of Emerging Technologies in Accounting* 13(1): 1–15.

Dai, J., and M.A. Vasarhelyi. 2017. "Toward Blockchain-Based Accounting and Assurance." *Journal of Information Systems* 31(3): 5–21. https://doi.org/10.2308/isys-51804.

DeCovny, S. 2012. "The Financial Psychopath Next Door." *CFA Institute Magazine* 23(2): 34–5.

Dellaportas, S. 2013. "Conversations With Inmate Accountants: Motivation, Opportunity and the Fraud Triangle." *Accounting Forum* 37(1): 29–39.

Deloitte. 2016a. "Blockchain Technology A Game Changer in Accounting?" Accessed March 21, 2018. www2.deloitte.com/content/dam/Deloitte/de/Documents/Innovation/Blockchain_A%20game-changer%20in%20accounting.pdf.

Deloitte. 2016b. "Blockchain- Enigma. Paradox. Opportunity." Accessed March 21, 2018. www2.deloitte.com/content/dam/Deloitte/uk/Documents/Innovation/deloitte-uk-Blockchain-full-report.pdf.

Deloitte. 2016c. "Bitcoin, Blockchain & Distributed Ledgers: Caught between Promise and Reality." www2.deloitte.com/content/dam/Deloitte/au/Images/infographics/au-deloittetechnology-bitcoin-Blockchain-distributed-ledgers-180416.pdf.

Deloitte. 2016d. "Tech Trends 2016: Innovating in the Digital Era: Blockchain: Democratised Trust Distributed Ledgers and the Future of Value." Accessed March 21, 2018. www2.deloitte.com/content/dam/Deloitte/uk/Documents/technology/deloitte-uk-techtrends-2016-blockchain.pdf.

Deloitte. 2018. "Blockchain: Opportunities for Health Care A New Model for Health Information Exchanges." Accessed December, 2020. www2.deloitte.com/us/en/pages/public-sector/articles/blockchainopportunities-for-health-care.

Digital Asset. 2016. "The Digital Asset Platform: Non-Technical White Paper." *Digital Asset Asset Holdings, LLC.* https://hub.digitalasset.com/hubfs/Documents/Digital%20Asset%20Platform%20-%20Non-technical%20White%20Paper.pdf.

Dorminey, J., A. Fleming, M. Kranacher, and R. Riley. 2012. "The Evolution of Fraud Theory." *Issues in Accounting Education* 27(2): 555–79.

Dorminey, J., S. Fleming, M. Kranacher, and R. Riley. 2011. "The Evolution of Fraud Theory." *American Accounting Association Annual Meeting,* 1–58. Denver.

Dorminey, J.W., S.A. Fleming, M.J. Kranacher, and R.A. Rilley. 2010. "Beyond the Fraud Triangle: Enhancing Deterrence of Economic Crimes." *The CPA Journal* 80(7): 17–23.

Dunn, P. 1999. *Fraudulent Financial Reporting: A Deception Based on Predisposition, Motive, and Opportunity.* PhD Thesis. Boston University, Graduate School of Management.

Epstein, B.J., and S. Ramamoorti. 2016. "Auditing With 'Dark Triad' Individuals in the Executive Ranks." *The CPA Journal* 86(3): 14–21.

EY. 2017. "The Risks and Opportunities of Blockchain Disruption in the Boardroom." Accessed December, 2019. www.ey.com/gl/en/issues/governance-and-reporting/center-for-boardmatters/ey-the-risks-and-opportunities-of-blockchain.

EY. 2018a. "Blockchain has the Potential to Streamline and Accelerate Business Processes and Reduce Risk." Accessed April 1, 2019. www.ey.com/en_gl/blockchain.

EY. 2021. "How AI Will Enable Us to Work Smarter, Faster." Accessed February 10, 2022. https://www.ey.com/en_fi/insights/assurance/how-ai-will-enable-us-to-work-smarter-faster.

Financial Services Authority. 2009. "The Turner Review a Regulatory Response to the Global Banking Crisis." Accessed April 20, 2018. www.nottingham.ac.uk/business/businesscentres/gcbfi/documents/researchreports/paper61.pdf.

Financial Stability Board. 2017. "Financial Stability Implications from FinTech." Accessed April 20, 2018. www.fsb.org/wp-content/uploads/R270617.pdf.

Financial Times. 2019. "Wirecard: The FT Guides Readers through the Accounting Scandal." https://enterprise.ft.com/en-gb/blog/wirecard-ft-guides-readers-through-accounting-scandal/.

Financial Times. 2020. "Wirecard and Me: Dan McCrum on Exposing a Criminal Enterprise." www.ft.com/content/745e34a1-0ca7-432c-b062-950c20e41f03.

Fraser, I. 1993. "Triple-entry Bookkeeping: A Critique." *Accounting & Business Research* 23(90).

Frunza, M.C. 2016. *Solving Modern Crime in Financial Markets.* 1st ed. Elsevier. Oxford, UK.

Furnham, A., S.C. Richards, and D.L. Paulhus, 2013. "The Dark Triad of Personality: A 10-Year Review." *Social and Personality Psychology Compass* 7(3): 199–216.

Gettsburg College. 2020. "One Third of Your Life Is Spent at Work." *Gettysburg College.*

Gray, R., D. Owen, and C. Adams. 1996. *Accounting and Accountability; Changes and Challenges in Corporate Social and Environmental Reporting.* Harlow: Prentice Hall Europe.

Goleman, D. 1998. *Working with Emotional Intelligence.* Bantam Books.

Grigg, I. 2005. "Triple Entry Accounting. Systemics Inc." Accessed June, 2021 https://doi.org/10.13140/RG.2.2.12032.43524.

Ham, C., M.H. Lang, N. Seybert, and S. Wang. 2015. "CFO Narcissism and Financial Reporting Quality." Accessed December 25, 2017. http://dx.doi.org/10.2139/ssrn.2581157, https://papers.ssrn.com/sol3/papers.cfm?abstract_id=2581157.

Hare, RD. 1994, "Predators: The Disturbing World of the Psychopaths among Us." *Psychology Today* 27(1): 54–61.

Harvard Business Review. 2015. "Six Components of a Great Corporate Culture." hbr.org.

Hasnan, S., R.A. Rahman, and S. Mahenthiran. 2008. *Management Predisposition, Motive, Opportunity, and Earnings Management for Fraudulent Financial Reporting in Malaysia*, 1–47. Accessed May 1, 2019. www.ssrn.com.

Higson, A. 2011. "Is Scepticism Enough? The Application of "Critical Thinking" to External Auditing, BAFA Annual Conference." 12–14. April 2011. Aston.

Hochberg, Y.V., P. Sapienza, and A. Vissing-Jorgensen. 2009. "A Lobbying Approach to Evaluating the Sarbanes-Oxley Act of 2002." *Journal of Accounting Research* 47(2): 519–83.

Hochberg, Y.V., P. Sapienza, and L. Zingales. 2009. "Liquidity and Control: The Effects of the Sarbanes-Oxley Act on the Financial Markets." *The Journal of Finance* 64(6): 1951–92.

Hodge, M., and L. Reid. 1971. "The Influence of Similarity between Relevant and Irrelevant Information Upon a Complex Identification Task." *Perception and Psychophysics* 10(4): 193–96.

Hollinger, R.C., and J.P. Clark. 1984. *Theft by Employees*. Lexington: Lexington Books.

Hyperledger. 2016. "Hyperledger Whitepaper." https://blockchainlab.com/pdf/Hyperledger%20Whitepaper.pdf.

IAASB. 2016. "Exploring the Growing Use of Technology in the Audit, with a Focus on Data Analytics." *IAASB Data Analytics Working Group*. Accessed April 20, 2018. www.accountancyeurope.eu/wp-content/uploads/IAASBs-Discussion-Paper-on-theuse-of-Technology-with-a-focus-on-Data-Analytics.pdf.iaa

IBM. 2012. "The Four V's of Big Data." Accessed April 20, 2018. www.ibmbigdatahub.com/infographic/four-vsbig- data.

IFAC. 2019. *Handbook of the International Code of Ethics for Professional Accountants (including International Independence Standards)*. New York: International Federation of Accountants. Accessed February 10, 2024. https://www.ifac.org.

Ijiri, Y. 1986. "A Framework for Triple Entry Bookkeeping." *The Accounting Review* 61(4): 745–759.

International Federation of Accountants. 2019. "International Code of Ethics for Professional Accountants (Including International Independence Standards." Accessed April 1, 2019. www.ethicsboard.org/publications/final-pronouncement-restructured-code-19.

Jackson, C.W. 2015. *Detecting Accounting Fraud. Analysis and Ethics*. Global ed. Ashford, UK: Pearson.

Jackson, K.E. 2015. *Accounting, Fraud, and Ethical Challenges in the Wake of the Financial Crisis*. New York: Cambridge University Press.

Jensen, M.C., and M.H. Meckling. 1976. "Theory of the Firm: Managerial Behavior, Agency Costs and Ownership Structure." *Journal of Financial Economics* 3(4): 305–60.

Kahn, W.A., and K.E. Kram. 1994. "Mentoring Relationships in Organizations: Lessons from the Past, Challenges for the Future." *Academy of Management Perspectives* 8(4): 24–37.

Kaptein, M. 2011. "Understanding Unethical Behaviour by Unravelling Ethical Culture." *Human Relations* 64(6): 843–69.

Kassem, R. 2016. *Detecting Financial Reporting Fraud: The Impact and Implications of Management Motivations for External Auditors – Evidence from the Egyptian Context.* PhD Thesis. https://repository.lboro.ac.uk/articles/ Detecting_financial_reporting_fraud_the_impact_and_implications_of_ management_motivations_for_external_auditors_-_evidence_from_the_ Egyptian_context/94960.

Kassem, R., and A. Higson. 2012. "Financial Reporting Fraud: Are Standards' Setters and Auditors Doing Enough?" *International Journal of Business and Social Science* 3(19): 283–90.

Kassem, R., and A.W. Higson. 2016. "External Auditors and Corporate Corruption: Implications for Audit Regulators." *Current Issues in Auditing.*

Koshy, P., D. Koshy, and P. McDaniel. 2014. "An Analysis of Anonymity in Bitcoin Using P2P Network Traffic." In *Financial Cryptography and Data Security,* edited by. N. Christin and R. Safavi-Naini. 8437. Lecture Notes in Computer Science. Heidelberg: Springer Berlin.

KPMG Forensic. 2014. *Fraud Risk Management: Developing a Strategy for Prevention, Detection, and Response.* Australia: KPMG.

KPMG. 2006. *Fraud Survey 2006.* Australia: KPMG Forensic.

KPMG. 2016a. *Fraud and Misconduct: The Changing Landscape.* Australia: KPMG.

KPMG. 2016b. *Consensus, Immutable Agreement for the Internet of Value.* Australia: KPMG.

KPMG. 2016c. *Leveraging Data Analytics and Continuous Auditing Processes for Improved Audit Planning, Effectiveness, and Efficiency.* Australia: KPMG.

KPMG. 2017a. *Audit 2025, The Future Is Now.* Forbes Insights (March). Australia: KPMG.

KPMG. 2017b. *KPMG Fraud Barometer 2017.* Australia: KPMG.

KPMG. 2018a. "Audit Point of View the Blockchain Shift will be Seismic." Accessed March, 2021. https://assets.kpmg/content/dam/kpmg/ca/ pdf/2018/02/apov-blockchain-feb-2018.pdf.

KPMG. 2018b. "Blockchain and the Future of Finance." Accessed March, 2021. https://advisory.kpmg.us/content/dam/advisory/en/pdfs/blockchain-future-finance.pdf.

Kranacher, M.J., R. Riley, and J.T. Wells. 2010. *Forensic Accounting and Fraud Examination,* 1st ed. John Hoboken, New Jersey, NJ: Wiley & Sons.

Lansiti, M., and K. Lakhani. 2017. "The Truth About Blockchain." *Harvard Business Review*: 3–11.

Le Maux, J., and D. Morin. 2011. "Black and White and Red All Over: Lehman Brothers' Inevitable Bankruptcy Splashed Across Its Financial Statements." *International Journal of Business & Social Science* 2(20): 39–48.

Lee, K., and M.C. Ashton. 2005. "Psychopathy, Machiavellianism, and Narcissism in the Five-Factor Model and the HEXACO Model of Personality Structure." *Personality and Individual Differences* 38: 1571–82.

Lerner, J.S., and P.E. Tetlock. 1999. "Accounting for the Effects of Accountability." *Psychological Bulletin* 125(2): 255–75. https://doi.org/10.1037/0033-2909. 125.2.255.

Lister, L.M. December 2007. "A Practical Approach to Fraud Risk." *Internal Auditor* 64(6): 1–30, December.

Loebbecke, J.K., M.M. Eining, and J.J. Willingham. 1989. "Auditor's Experience with Material Irregularities: Frequency, Nature, and Detectability." *Auditing: A Journal of Practice & Theory* 9(1): 1–28, Fall.

Lokanan, M.E. 2015. "Challenges to the Fraud Triangle: Questions on Its Usefulness." *Accounting Forum* 39(3): 201–24.

Marks, J. 2009. *Playing Offense in a High-Risk Environment.* New York: Crowe Horwath.

Mayer-Schönberger, V., and K. Cukier. 2013. *Big Data: A Revolution That Will Transform How We Live, Work, and Think.* New York, MA: Eamon Dolan/ Houghton Mifflin Harcourt.

McDonalds. 2019. "Standards of Business Conduct." www.google.co.uk/url?s a=i&rct=j&q=&esrc=s&source=web&cd=&cad=rja&uact=8&ved=0CAQ Qw7AJahcKEwjY9PGbl6f-AhUAAAAAHQAAAAAQAw&url=https%3 A%2F%2Fcorporate.mcdonalds.com%2Fcontent%2Fdam%2Fsites%2F corp%2Fnfl%2Fpdf%2FUK-English_Standards_of_Business_Conduct_ December_2019.pdf&psig=AOvVaw3BkRK8TjMZ-0YC1bn2P0Ep&u st=1681486299610264.

McGuire, D., and Hutchings, K. 2006. "A Machiavellian Analysis of Organizational Change." *Journal of Organization Change Management* 19(2): 192–209.

Mckee, M., and R. Santore. 2008. "Hand in the Cookie Jar: An Experimental Investigation of Equity-Based Compensation and Managerial Fraud." *Southern Economic Journal* 75(1): 261–78.

Mokhiber, R. 2007. "Twenty Things You Should Know About Corporate Crime." *Inc: Taming the Giant Corporation Conference.* Washington, DC.

Morales, J., Y. Gendron, and H. Guénin-Paracini. 2014. "The Construction of the Risky Individual and Vigilant Organization: A Genealogy of the Fraud Triangle." *Accounting, Organizations and Society* 39(3): 170–94.

Murphy, P.R., and M.T. Dacin. 2011. "Psychological Pathways to Fraud: Understanding and Preventing Fraud in Organisations." *Journal of Business Ethics* 101: 601–18.

Nakamoto, S. 2008. "Bitcoin: A peer-to-peer Electronic Cash System." Bitcoin: A Peer-to-Peer Electronic Cash System (researchgate.net). Accessed July, 2021.

Nicodemus. A. 2020. "Automate Your Accounting Processes to Wring Out Fraud." *Blackline e-book.*

Nicodemus, A. 2021. "Want to Wring Out Fraud? Automate Your Accounting Processes." *Compliance Week*, June 29. Accessed February 10, 2024. https://www.complianceweek.com/accounting-and-auditing/want-to-wring-out-fraud-automate-your-accounting-processes/30512.article.

Nijenhuis, R. 2016. *Prevention of Fraud Cases.* MBA Thesis. University of Twente. https://essay.utwente.nl/69819/1/Nijenhuis_MA_BMS.pdf.

Ogutu, E.O. 2016. "Corporate Failure and the Role of Governance: The Parmalat Scandal." *International Journal of Management and Information Technology* 11(3): 2747–54.

Paulhus, D.L., and K.M. Williams. 2002. *"The Dark Triad of Personality." Journal of Research in Personality* 36: 556–63.

Perols, J.L., and B.A. Lougee. 2010. "The Relation between Earnings Management and Financial Statement Fraud." *Advances in Accounting, Incorporating Advances in International Accounting.* Accessed March 1, 2019. www.elsevier.com.

PwC. 2017. "Distributed Ledger Technology—The Genesis of a New Business Model for the Asset Management Industry." Accessed April 27, 2018. www.pwc.lu/en/fintech/docs/pwcfintech-distributed-ledger-technology.pdf.

Ramamoorti, S. 2008. "The Psychology and Sociology of Fraud: Integrating the Behavioural Sciences Component into Fraud and Forensic Accounting Curricula." *Issues in Accounting Education* 23(4): 521–33.

Ramamoorti, S., D. Morrison, and J.W. Koletar. 2009. "Bringing Freud to Fraud: Understanding the State of Mind of the C-level Suite/White Collar Offender through A-B-C Analysis." *The Institute for Fraud Prevention (IFP)*: 1–35.

Rezaee, Z. 2003. *Financial Statement Fraud: Prevention and Detection.* New York: Wiley.

Rezaee, Z. 2005. "Causes, Consequences, and Deterrence of Financial Statement Fraud." *Critical Perspectives on Accounting* 16: 227–98.

Rezaee, Z. 2005. "Causes, Consequences, and Detections of Financial Statement Fraud." *Research in Accounting Regulation* 18(1): 147–70. https://doi.org/10.1016/S1052-0457(05)18008-7.

Rezaee, Z., and R. Riley. 2010. *Financial Statement Fraud: Prevention and Detection.* 2nd ed. Hoboken, NJ: John Wiley & Sons, Inc.

Roberts, B.W., K.E. Walton, and W. Viechtbauer. 2006. "Patterns of Mean-Level Change in Personality Traits Across the Life Course: A Meta-Analysis of Longitudinal Studies." *Psychological Bulletin* 132(1): 1–25.

Rumi, J.A. (Translated by Coleman Barks). *1995. The Essential Rumi.* HarperOne.

Schnatterly, K. 2010. "Increasing Firm Value Through Detection and Prevention of White-collar Crime." In *Handbook of Top Management Teams*, edited by F. Bournois, J. Duval-Hamel, S. Roussillon, and J.L. Scaringella. UK: Palgrave Macmillan, London.

Schrand, C.M., and S.L. Zechman. 2012. "Executive Overconfidence and the Slippery Slope to Financial Misreporting." *Journal of Accounting and Economics* 53(1): 311–29.

SEC. 2003. "Report of Investigation by The Special Investigative Committee of the Board of Directors of Worldcom, Inc." Accessed November 16, 2018. www.sec.gov/Archives/edgar/data/723527/000093176303001862/dex991.htm.

Sheikh, F.M. 2017. *The Corporate Governance Cosmos*. Presentation. 3rd Annual MBA Symposium. Salford Business School. Salford. England.

Skousen, C.J., and C.J. Wright. 2006. "Contemporaneous Risk Factors and the Prediction of Financial Statement Fraud." Accessed July 31, 2018. www.ssrn.com.

SSRN. Accessed 22 December, 2017. http://dx.doi.org/10.2139/ssrn.2279976.

Stevens, G.W., J.K. Deuling, and A.A. Armenakis. 2012. "Successful Psychopaths: Are They Unethical Decision-Makers and Why?" *Journal of Business Ethics* 105: 139–49.

Swartz, M. 2003. *Power Failure: The Inside Story of the Collapse of Enron*. New York: Doubleday.

Szabo, N. 1994. "Smart contracts." Accessed October, 2020. www.fon.hum.uva.nl/rob/Courses/InformationInSpeech/CDROM/Literature/ LOTwinterschool2006/szabo.best.vwh.net/smart.contracts.html.

Tapscott, D., and A. Tapscott. 2016. "The Impact of the Blockchain Goes Beyond Financial Services." *Harvard Business Review Digital Articles*. https://hbr.org/2016/05/the-impact-of-the-blockchain-goes-beyond-financial-services.

The Financial Reporting Council. 2016. "The UK Code of Corporate Governance." Accessed January 1, 2019. www.frc.gov.uk, www.frc.org.uk/getattachment/ca7e94c4-b9a9-49e2-a824-ad76a322873c/UK-Corporate-Governance-Code-April-2016.pdf.

The Guardian. 2017. Accessed September 1, 2019. www.theguardian.com/business/2017/mar/28/tesco-agrees-fine-serious-fraud-office-accounting-scandal.

The Japan News. 2015. ¥7.3 Billion Fine Sought for Toshiba Over Accounting Fraud. December 8. www.japantimes.co.jp/news/2015/12/25/business/corporate-business/toshiba-fined-record-%C2%A57-3-billion-over-accounting-scandal/.

Trevino, L.K., M. Brown, and L.P. Hartman. 2006. "A Qualitative Investigation of Perceived Executive Ethical Leadership: Perceptions from Inside and Outside the Executive Suite." *Human Relations* 56(1): 5–3.

U.S. General Accounting Office. (2002). *Financial Statement Restatements: Trends, Market Impacts, Regulatory Responses, and Remaining Challenges (GAO-03-138)*. Washington, D.C.: U.S. Government Printing Office.

Van Vlasselaer, V., T. Eliassi-Rad, L. Akoglu, M. Snoeck, and B. Baesens. 2016. "Gotcha! Network-based Fraud Detection for Social Security Fraud." *Management Science* 63(9): 2773–3145.

Wall Street Journal. 2012. "Psychos on Wall Street." Accessed December 24, 2017. http://on.wsj.com/1mxrhIY.

Warren, J.D. Jr., K.C. Moffitt, and P. Byrnes. 2015. "How Big Data Will Change Accounting." *Accounting Horizons* 29(2): 397–407.

Well, A.D. 1971. "The Influence of Irrelevant Information on Speeded Classification Tasks." *Perception and Psychophysics* 10(2): 79–84.

Wells, J.T. 2011. *Financial Statement Fraud Casebook: Baking the Ledgers and Cooking the Books.* Hoboken, NY: John Wiley & Sons.

Wolfe, D.T., and D.R. Hermanson. 2004 "The Fraud Diamond: Considering the Four Elements of Fraud." *The CPA Journal* 74(12): 38–42.

Woodcock, D. 2015. "Accounting Fraud: Down, But Not Out." *Law 360.* New York. *www.jonesday.com/accounting-fraud-down-but-not-out-ilaw-360i-09-11-2015.*

Woodward, J.D. Jr., N.M. Orlans, and P.T. Higgins. 2003. *Biometrics: Identity Assurance in the Information Age.* Santa Monica, CA: McGraw-Hill.

Wright, T. 2022. "Blockchain Analytics Unable to Prevent FTX-level Illicit Schemes." *Cointelegraph*, December 1. Accessed February 2024. https://cointelegraph.com/news/blockchain-analytics-unable-to-prevent-ftx-level-illicit-schemes.

Yu, T., Z. Lin, and Q. Tang. 2018. Blockchain: Introduction and Application in Financial Accounting. Accessed July, 2021. doi:10.2139/ssrn.3258504.

Zahra, S.A., R.L. Priem, and A.A. Rasheed. 2005. "The Antecedents and Consequences of Top Management Fraud." *Journal of Management* 31(6): 803–28.

Zhang, J., X. Yang, and D. Appelbaum. 2015. "Toward Effective Big Data Analysis in Continuous Auditing." *Accounting Horizons* 29(2): 469–76.

About the Authors

Dr. Faisal Sheikh, FCCA, spent more than a decade in audit assurance and business advisory. Faisal is an established academic and award-winning financial reporting teacher, and his research interests include forensic accounting and generative AI. This book marks his fourth publication with Business Expert Press.

Saad Maniar, FCCA, is a senior partner and board member at Crowe UAE (set to lead Baker Tilly in the Gulf from July 2025), an acclaimed practitioner and thought leader with a track record of more than 25 years in audit assurance, taxation, and business advisory. Saad also chairs the UAE ACCA Members Advisory Committee, representing over 10,000 aspiring and working professionals.

Index

www.ingramcontent.com/pod-product-compliance
Lightning Source LLC
Jackson TN
JSHW082059240825
89831JS00007B/70

9 7 8 1 6 3 7 4 2 7 6 0 6